NINETEENTH-CENTURY COSTUME AND FASHION

HERBERT NORRIS AND OSWALD CURTIS

Illustrated by
Oswald Curtis

DOVER PUBLICATIONS, INC.
Mineola, New York

Copyright

Publisher's Note copyright © 1998 by Dover Publications, Inc.
All rights reserved under Pan American and International Copyright Conventions.

Published in Canada by General Publishing Company, Ltd., 30 Lesmill Road, Don Mills, Toronto, Ontario.
Published in the United Kingdom by Constable and Company, Ltd., 3 The Lanchesters, 162–164 Fulham Palace Road, London W6 9ER.

Bibliographical Note

This Dover edition, first published in 1998, is an unabridged republication of the work originally published in 1933 by E. P. Dutton and Co., Inc., New York, under the title *Costume and Fashion, Volume Six: The Nineteenth Century*.

Library of Congress Cataloging-in-Publication Data

Norris, Herbert.
   [Costume & fashion. V. 6, Nineteenth century]
   Nineteenth-century costume and fashion / Herbert Norris and Oswald Curtis ; illustrated in color & black and white by Oswald Curtis.
        p.   cm.
   Originally published: Costume & fashion. V. 6, Nineteenth century. New York : E.P. Dutton, 1933.
   ISBN 0-486-40292-4 (pbk.)
   1. Costume—History—19th century.   I. Curtis, Oswald.
II. Title.
GT720.N62   1998
391'.009'034—dc21
                                                                98-9926
                                                                CIP

Manufactured in the United States of America
Dover Publications, Inc., 31 East 2nd Street, Mineola, N.Y. 11501

PUBLISHER'S NOTE

Herbert Norris was renowned in his time as a costume architect and archaeologist. He designed historical and theatrical costume and stage sets for one hundred plays in England and America, as well as for a number of British films and pageants. Nevertheless, his series of books, *Costume and Fashion,* is considered his finest achievement.

Originally intended to be a six-volume series that would tell the story of costume and fashion from the time of ancient Greece until the end of the nineteenth century, only four volumes were completed and published before his death in 1950. They include *Volume 1: The Evolution of European Dress through the Earlier Ages* (1924); *Volume 2: Senlac to Bosworth, 1066–1485* (1927); *Volume 3: The Tudors, 1485–1603,* 2 vols. (1938); and *Volume 6: The Nineteenth Century* (1933), with Oswald Curtis, of which this book is the unabridged reprint. (The reader may notice a few references to the earlier volumes in the text of this work.) The fourth and fifth volumes, if completed, would have covered the Stuart and Hanoverian periods of fashion history, respectively.

Volumes 1 and 2 of the series are currently out of print, while Volume 3 is available in a one-volume (unabridged) Dover edition published in 1997. It combines Books I and II of the original work, and is entitled *Tudor Costume and Fashion* (ISBN 0-486-29845-0).

It should also be noted here that of the four volumes completed, only the current volume features the illustrations of Oswald Curtis; in the previous works, Mr. Norris acted as his own illustrator. In this single instance, the English publisher arranged a collaboration, since—as was noted in the Foreword to the original edition reprinted here—Mr. Curtis already had a considerable collection of material relating to nineteenth-century costume.

FOREWORD

IT is my desire to continue the series of volumes on 'Costume and Fashion' up to the present day. Volume III, The Tudors, is nearing completion and will be published within the next eighteen months. Volume IV, The Stuarts, and Volume V, The Hanoverians, will follow in due course.

As Mr. Oswald Curtis had already collected a great deal of material referring to nineteenth-century costume, the publishers arranged a collaboration so that his work on this period should be published as a part of my own series. Hence Volume VI. Most of the descriptions of clothes and all the excellent drawings are by Mr. Curtis. The text relating to historical facts, social life, and the more practical side of the subject is my own.

The plan of arrangement of Volumes I and II has been followed as far as possible, but the periods treated in the present volume differ so much that it has not been found practicable to do this entirely.

The appreciation of Volumes I and II by the public and press has made me venture to hope that the present effort will prove of equal value.

HERBERT NORRIS.

THAME, OXON, 1933.

PUBLISHER'S NOTE

Owing to the illness of Mr. Curtis, the entire responsibility for reading the proofs and preparing this volume for the press has been undertaken by Mr. Norris.

CONTENTS

LIST OF ILLUSTRATIONS

COLOUR PLATES

Note: For this edition, all the color plates appear between pages 120 and 121.

LIST OF ILLUSTRATIONS

BLACK AND WHITE

SOME AUTHORITIES QUOTED

Dr. E. Barthez
Max von Boehn
A. de Burgh
Sir Bernard Burke
Lady Charlotte Bury
E. A. Campbell
Countess of Cardigan
Dr. E. Willett Cunnington
Dr. Oskar Fischel
Joseph Haydn
Friedrich Hottenroth
Talbot Hughes
Robert Huish
Elizabeth Jenkins
Clare Jerrold
Carl Köhler

Lewis Melville
Lady Dorothy Nevill
Ralph Nevill
Auguste Racinet
House of Reville
Lytton Strachey
Grace E. Thompson
Alice M. Wilson
Jean Philippe Worth
Maison Worth

Biographies
Contemporary Letters
      ,,   Journals
      ,,   Magazines
      ,,   Newspapers

CHAPTER I

THE LATTER PART OF THE REIGN OF GEORGE III
(1800–20); THE REGENCY (1810–20)

CONTEMPORARY FOREIGN GOVERNMENTS

FRANCE: The Consulate (1799–1804)
The First Empire, Napoleon I (1804–14)
Louis XVIII, King of France (1814–24)

PRUSSIA: Frederick William III (1797–1840)

AUSTRIA: Francis I (1804–35)

RUSSIA: Paul I (1796–1801)
Alexander I (1801–25)

SPAIN: Charles IV (1788–1808)
Joseph Bonaparte (1808–14)
Ferdinand VII (1814–33)

ITALY: Napoleon I, King of Italy (1805–14)

INTRODUCTION

KING GEORGE III was little seen in public during the last twenty years of his reign, nor did he take part in any important regal ceremonials.

The Act of Union of the three nations, England, Scotland, and Ireland, was passed in 1800, and the Royal Proclamation setting forth the design for the Union Jack, as used ever since, was issued on 1st January 1801. Public interest was much excited at this time by an alarming illness of His Majesty. In October 1810 a most serious disorder overtook him, and it was necessary that George, Prince of Wales, should be entrusted with the Regency. The final ceremonial of the Prince's investiture took place on 5th February 1811. 'It was observed on this occasion, that the Regent's conduct was dignified in the extreme', although later it was stated that '1811 opened brightly with the antics of the new Prince Regent and his costly entertainments'.

During the first twenty years of the nineteenth century there was a marked deterioration in social manners and morals, which were no longer influenced by the 'scrupulous observance of propriety of conduct'

I

of Queen Charlotte's Court. In this connection a letter-writer of 1815 states:

The affectation of domestic manners and customs has for about a year been totally laid aside. Luxury and all its attendants are as prevalent as in former days; but the imposing splendour of rank, and the polished manners of the ancient nobility, which in some degree softened the rude features of vice, are now exchanged for splendour without taste, and pride without dignity.

In 1815 it was rumoured that Queen Charlotte would hold a Drawing Room, 'the object being instigated by a desire to slight Caroline, Princess of Wales'. The following excerpt from a letter written at the time explains the situation more succinctly:

This great event was settled the other day at Carlton House. The old Queen did not like it at first, or pretended not to do so, but was at last obliged to consent. . . . The thing is so extraordinary! That an old Dowager Queen—for, in fact, she is a Dowager as long as the poor king is set aside, from a living death—that she, I say, should give a Drawing-Room and gaieties, when there is a Princess Regent whose business it is to do so.

During the reign of George III, Drawing Rooms were held in the evening at St. James's Palace, when the State apartments, lit by hundreds of wax candles, made a splendid setting for the brilliant costumes and uniforms. In the early part of the nineteenth century, candles were, of course, the only means of illumination in households of every class. Only the well-to-do, however, used candles of wax, the humbler households being forced to employ those of mutton-fat, dips and rushlights.

Lighting by gas was first used, but in an exceptional instance, in 1792. The London and Westminster Gaslight Company was incorporated in 1810. In 1813 certain London streets were lighted by gas in place of oil lamps. Neither gas nor oil was yet employed for indoor illumination.

Under the guidance of the immaculate Beau Brummell the Prince Regent's influence on masculine dress was considerable; in fact it is said that he took infinitely more interest in the visits of his tailor than in those of his ministers.

Fig. 1 is a drawing made from a portrait of George as Prince Regent. He wears a double-breasted TAIL-COAT buttoned very tightly round his opulent figure, and having velvet lapels and close-fitting sleeves. The rather short-waisted coat shows the points of the waist-coat. Light knee-breeches are worn over silk stockings and pumps. Other accessories are the neckcloth, Star of the Garter, FOB, and CHAPEAU BRAS carried under the arm. The hair is wavy and dressed rather high.

MEN'S COSTUME

It is generally believed that France led the fashions in the nineteenth century, therefore it is interesting to learn that such was not entirely

Fig. 1. The Prince Regent

the case where men's clothes were concerned. Beau Brummell was famous as a leader of fashion in England. He was a supreme example of that class known as the dandy, a name which came into general use at the beginning of the nineteenth century.

George Bryan Brummell was born in 1778 and educated at Eton (1790) and at Oriel College, Oxford. 'The best scholar, the best boatman, the best cricketer. . . . Tall, well made, with a good figure, he affected an old-world air of courtesy.'

Brummell first came to the notice of the Prince of Wales while at college, and received from his Royal Highness a commission in his own regiment.[1] From an early age it was his ambition to be the best dressed man in London, and from 1794 to 1816 he reigned as absolute Monarch of the Mode.

The first to discard powder for the hair, 'Brummell used his influence to simplify costume. He was the quietest, plainest, and most unpretentious dresser. He eschewed colours, trinkets, and gewgaws; his clothes were exquisitely made, and, above all, adapted to his person; he put them on well, too', said Lord William Pitt Lennox, one of the many leaders of society with whom the Beau was well acquainted. 'The Fashionable bowed before his creaseless coat and his artistic, neat-folded cravat.' He introduced starch into his neckcloth. A volume on the subject with practical instructions and illustrations was published at the time under the title 'Neckclothiana'. The Prince Regent wept bitter tears when Brummell disapproved the cut of the royal coat!

During the day, Beau Brummell appeared in a blue coat with brass buttons, a light or buff-coloured waistcoat, and deep, stiff, white cravat; PANTALOONS or buckskin breeches with HESSIANS or top-boots. At night he wore a blue coat, white waistcoat, and white cravat, black stockinet pantaloons buttoned tight round the ankle over striped silk socks, and low, black, highly varnished shoes. Knee-breeches and *chapeau bras* (see page 15) were only used at Court, the Opera, or Almack's—a suite of assembly rooms in King Street, St. James's, built in 1765 by Mr. M'Call and much patronized by fashionable men and women for more than a century. Later they were known as Willis's Rooms. Beau Brummell was also considered an authority on all matters concerning polite society, and he was responsible for making Brighthelmstone a fashionable seaside resort. His meteoric and glorious career, however, ended sadly, for he later became insane, and in 1840 died a pauper.

COATS AND OVERCOATS. At the beginning of the nineteenth century, clothes generally had undergone a considerable change as a result of the French Revolution, which affected modes and costumes in many countries beyond France. The DRESS COAT proper, which was so

---

[1] The Tenth Hussars.

characteristic of the eighteenth century, went out of fashion in 1792, except as Court dress, at St. James's Palace on State occasions (see Fig. 2). Fig. 3 is a diagram of the dress coat. The two fronts and the two backs are shown, and half the collar. A B and J I are the shoulders.

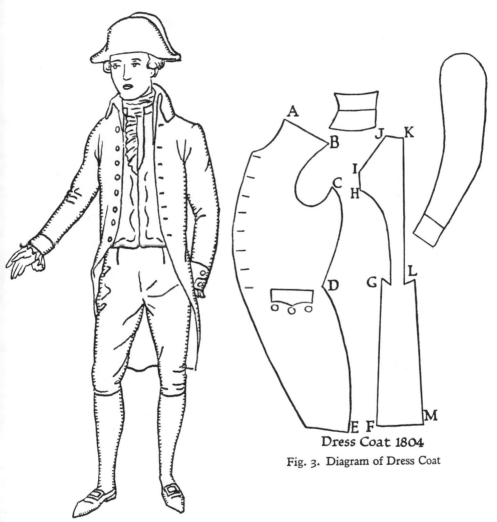

Dress Coat 1804

Fig. 3. Diagram of Dress Coat

Fig. 2. The Dress Coat 1800

C D and H G is the side seam under the arm. From D E the coat is left open and the portion of the back G F is the under-flap. The centre seam down the back is shown in K L. The same under-flap down the centre of the tail is shown in L M. The sleeve is shaped to the ordinary pattern, and the cuff is but a close fold back. The top of the pocket-

flap is almost level with the waist. For a description of COURT DRESS
see Chapter V, page 142. Napoleon I reintroduced the dress-coat in
his Court after his coronation as Emperor in 1804. In cut, however,
it showed distinct traces of revolutionary influence.

turnover
collar

1808-20

Fig. 5. Diagram of Coat

Fig. 4. Gentleman 1804

Fig. 6. Diagram of General Sleeve

The JEAN DE BRY COAT was introduced from France in 1799.
It was short-waisted, fastened with three buttons, with small revers and
a stand-up velvet collar. From the front the coat was cut away in a
curve to the short, pointed tails at the back, where the narrow pocket-
flaps were set close together. The sleeves were close fitting except on

the shoulders, where they were padded, and two buttons fastened them close round, and well over the hand.   Between the coat and the trousers was seen the waistcoat of some fancy material.

In Fig. 4 is shown a fashionably dressed man of the early years of the century. He wears a double-breasted *tail-coat* cut as diagram (Fig. 5), with short-waisted waistcoat and close-fitting breeches. The rather floppy ties at the knee and the handkerchief carelessly hanging from the coat pocket are a survival of the revolutionary era. The seams on the shoulders under the arms, and the flap down the sides and centre back, are constructed in the same manner as in Fig. 3. Notice should be taken of the darts at the neck and at the waist-line. Fig. 6 shows the diagram of cut of the sleeve in general use, and can be used with all coats where no diagram of a sleeve is shown.

In 1800, an English overcoat called the GARRICK came into vogue. This garment, with its numerous capes, sometimes as many as four being added, was a sort of hybrid coat and cloak (see Plate I), and it entirely superseded the eighteenth-century cloak except for travelling purposes.

The year 1805 saw the introduction of another English overcoat, the SPENCER, of somewhat extraordinary design. This fashionable short coat, with two little tabs below the waist-line at the back, was named after the second Earl Spencer, K.G. (1758–1834), who was thrown whilst taking a hedge in the hunting field. His coat-tails were caught in the briers and torn off short. This event inspired the following lines:

> Two noble Earls whom, if I quote,
> Some folks might call me sinner,
> The one invented half a coat,
> The other half a dinner.

The latter reference is to John, third Earl of Sandwich, diplomat and statesman (1748–92), a sorry rake and profligate, who invented the edible of that name to save himself the trouble of rising from the gaming-table to take a more substantial meal.

The Spencer had very short sleeves and no tails, being made to protect only the upper part of the body. To heighten this curious effect, it was made of light-coloured cloth in contrast to the darker coat worn beneath. This novel overcoat was a sort of pendant to the Spencer bodice worn by ladies at this period.

The *broad-tailed English* RIDING COAT (called 'REDINGOTE' in France), often worn instead of the dress-coat, was not in general use until 1810.

Another coat which was popular from 1807 was the POLISH COAT, with its distinctive ornamentation of cord and tassels (Fig. 7).

Fig. 8 shows the cut of the Polish coat, but with shorter skirts. In the longer form of this coat the skirts radiate out from A and B and

collar

Fig. 8. Diagram of Polish Coat

Fig. 7. The Polish Coat 1815

consequently are wider at the bottom hem, which naturally falls into many more folds. The pattern of the back is detached from the skirt part and is pleated at the waist-line. Collars of the Polish coat varied: some were upstanding as in Fig. 7, others folded back and were cut as shown in diagram (Fig. 8).

Coats in general sported very high turnover collars and wide-shaped

lapels.   The front of the coat was double-breasted and cut away at
the waist in a short square, leaving a long-tailed skirt behind (see Fig. 7,
and Plate II).   The sleeves were full at the shoulders (see Fig. 6,
dotted extensions), tightening on the forearm, and ending in a cuff

Fig. 9. Gentleman 1812

or buttoned cuff-shape at the wrist.   Fig. 9 shows the novel cut of the
back of a similar coat, and also the pleats required in the armhole to
give even fuller sleeves than those previously noticed.   *Overcoats* were
both double- and single-breasted; sometimes the sleeves had a turn-up
cuff, sometimes a sewn-on cuff.

By 1818 the shoulders of the *dress coat* had broadened.   The coat now stood away from the body at the chest, but fitted closely above the hips. The tails were narrower and came well below the knees (see Plate III). The sleeves remained full at the shoulder and tight at the wrist, but widened again, curving over the hand as far as the fingers.

The following quotation under date 1818 is given as an example of the fantastic names applied to garments or parts of them: 'A *collar à la Guillotine*, to show the neck behind'.

The smartest coats worn in the second decade of the century fitted the masculine waist to perfection. Mr. Weston (1816), of Old Bond Street, had the reputation for the best cut for the long-tail and short-waisted coat. The fashionable colour for coats was sky-blue, more elegantly termed 'Bleu Céleste'. 'Mr. Ward had on his Bleu Céleste, both as to his coat and his temper.' This excerpt is from a letter dated 19th June 1814.

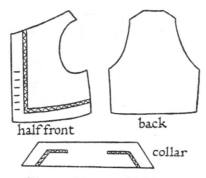

Fig. 10. Diagram of Waistcoat

Waistcoats were also worn double- and single-breasted, and the collar was sometimes broad and sometimes narrow. The deep collar was kept upright by thin whalebones sewn into the front edges (see Plate II, and Fig. 10). Later, a turn-down collar came into vogue (see Fig. 39, Chapter II). The bottom edge of the waistcoat was sometimes cut straight, sometimes into small tails or points. Very often more than one waistcoat was worn at the same time, the upper one being cut so as to show the top of the lower one (see Fig. 4). With regard to materials, a light-coloured cashmere, elaborately embroidered, was very popular, as were also striped or patterned materials. Waistcoats made of white *piqué* were fashionable in 1814 for evening wear. In 1818 broad-striped waistcoats were the mode for day wear in Paris. A fob was often worn hanging from beneath the waistcoat.

CLOAKS. During the severe winter of 1809 cloaks of fur were worn by many elegants. Although exciting a certain amount of ridicule from the man in the street, they remained in use to be donned in very cold weather or in the evening over full dress.

NECKWEAR. During the beginning of the nineteenth century, plain black or white STOCKS tied with a front bow were worn, with a starched or unstarched collar underneath. The points of the collar stood up on both sides of the face, a forerunner of what was known later as the CHOKER COLLAR. The low-cut waistcoat revealed a frilled or gathered shirt-front. A tie-pin was often worn in the centre of the stock or frilling. From 1818 the stock or neckcloth had a fairly broad lining, shaped at the sides and stiffened with whalebone or pigs' bristles to rise in an arch at the cheeks. For examples refer to the various figures.

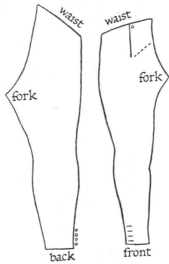

Fig. 11. Diagram of Ankle-length Breeches

'BREECHES', towards the end of the eighteenth century, grew longer and longer, until in 1800 they reached ankle-length. The lower part was usually hidden by boots or gaiters (see Plates I and II). Sometimes, however, the ankle-length breeches were worn over the boots (see Fig. 7). Fig. 11 is a diagram of the cut, and shows back and front of one leg of a pair of breeches. For dimensions of these garments refer to 'Costume and Fashion', Vol. II, p. 224. Breeches were made as tight-fitting as possible, of cloth, buckskin, or stockinette, generally of a light colour. In England, the front opening took the form of a flap about 1780, and this continued until nearly the middle of the nineteenth century. The front flap was sometimes elaborately embroidered with cord (see Fig. 12). The tight-fitting, ankle-length breeches were sometimes called PANTALETTES.

About 1812 TROUSERS (or pantaloons), somewhat wider than the breeches, appeared. They were secured by straps under the soles of the boots (see Plate III). These trousers very often came up nearly to the wearer's armpits. The draw-string round the waist previously in use

Fig. 12. Gentleman 1810

was now superseded by BRACES in the form of broad tapes passing over the shoulders and buttoned to the trousers both back and front. The wearing of this novelty so completely embarrassed a vehement orator that, overcome by nervousness and excitement, he unconsciously unbuttoned his braces, with disastrous results. As in the case of breeches, the front opening of the trousers at this time took the form of a flap. Fig. 13 is a diagram showing the cut of a pair of trousers.

Despite the introduction of trousers, *knee-breeches* continued in use, and were the only style for wear with the dress coat or at Court (see Figs. 2, 4, and 14).

The readoption of trousers dates from 1797, when Frederick William III of Prussia appeared in long trousers. Previously, as early as 1793, trousers had been worn, but the fashionable world

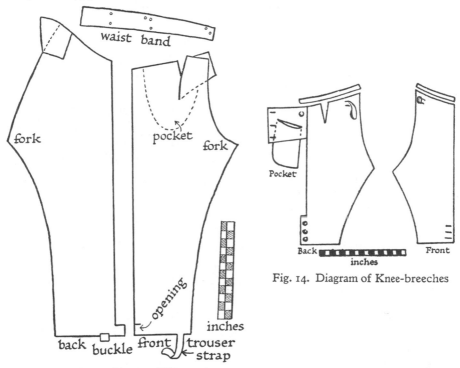

Fig. 14. Diagram of Knee-breeches

Fig. 13. Diagram of Trousers

at that time considered them a distasteful innovation. Now, how-ever, that royalty had condescended to wear them, it was decided that they must be tolerated.

Wide trousers were the national costume of the Venetians in the fifteenth century. St. Pantaleon was their patron saint, and many Venetians received this as a Christian name; consequently they were satirically termed 'Pantaloni' by the Italians. Pantaloon in Italian comedy was inspired by ridicule of the Venetians, and Jacques Callot, the French artist (1592–1635), painted Pantaloon wearing these wide trousers. English sailors of the sixteenth century were the first to revive the wearing of wide trousers.

Trousers were exceptional in England until Viscount Wellington introduced them into the army in 1806, during the Peninsular War. They were known as 'Wellington trousers'. After this they came into more general use, despite the tremendous outcry against them. Almack's, much patronized by the fashionable world, set its face against trousers, and those affecting such garments were refused admission. The universities were equally firm in their opposition. In 1812 the dons of Trinity and St. John's Colleges, Cambridge, ordained that any student wearing trousers or pantaloons in Chapel or Hall should be 'signed off' as absent.[1]

After Waterloo (1815) all the young swells of Paris wore trousers. When Beau Brummell returned to England from Paris in 1816 he received an invitation from Lady Hertford to her town-house in Manchester Square,[2] 'to have the honour of meeting the Prince Regent'. The Beau went dressed *à la française* in blue coat, white cravat and waistcoat, black trousers, shoes, and silk stockings. After he had made his reverence, one of the prince's gentlemen came to him: 'The Great Man is very much surprised that you should have ventured to appear in his presence without knee-breeches. He considers it as a want of proper respect to him'! Despite this Royal rebuke the Prince Regent appeared himself in trousers a month later, and Society followed the Prince's lead. The older generation, however, still favoured knee-breeches for day and evening wear. Up to 1870 some country gentlemen much past middle life still adhered to the old custom of wearing knee-breeches.

An item from a wardrobe account of a fashionable young man dated 1818 runs: 'A pair of PETERSHAM (see page 44) *pantaloons* with striped flounces at the bottom'.

FOOTWEAR. Boots of several varieties were worn. The top-boot with pointed or oval-shaped front and tassel, known as the 'Hessian boot' (see Plate I), vied with a boot having a longish brown top set fairly low on the leg (see Fig. 15). There was also an oval-toed low shoe in use. Shoes with buckles were still worn for ceremonial occasions (see Figs. 2 and 4). After the Battle of Waterloo in 1815, the names of both the allied generals, Marshal BLÜCHER and the Duke of WELLINGTON, were bestowed on different varieties of boots. *Gaiters* were sometimes worn, but chiefly in the country (see Plate II).

HEADGEAR. At the beginning of this period the same hats were worn as in the latter part of the eighteenth century; a front cockade

---

[1] In 1923 students of Trinity College were signed off for wearing 'plus fours' in Chapel or Hall.

[2] Hertford House, so often honoured with the presence of Beau Brummell and other leaders of fashion, and now the home of the Wallace Collection.

hat and a hat with rounded crown and rather wide brim (see Plate I).
The round hat, however, gained enormously in favour, and by 1812 was
the usual wear for the upper and middle classes throughout the whole
of Europe (see Figs. 7, 9, and 12).   The old three-cornered hat (or

Fig. 15. Gentleman 1820

Tricorne) completely disappeared, and the TOP HAT began its long and
varied career.   A form of *cocked hat*, with brim turned right up both
back and front, continued to be worn or carried with uniform or on
ceremonial occasions (see Figs. 2 and 4).   This was often called the
'*chapeau bras*'.

HAIRDRESSING. Wigs had ceased to be worn, except by elderly
people, at the close of the eighteenth century.   The fashion of

powdered hair had also gone out at the end of the French Revolution (1792). The hair was now worn short, but left rather full in front. Around the year 1806 the hair was cut quite close to the head, but by 1809 it was allowed to curl. A fascinating coiffure of this time was called '*en chérubin*', and needs no description. Curly hair continued to be worn by fashionable men for some length of time. Short *side-whiskers* were also worn (see 'Costume and Fashion', Vol. I, p. 49).

In France, the hair was sometimes cut in imitation of Greek and Roman statues, and the '*style à la Titus*', '*à la Brutus*', and other so-called classical modes were evolved.

FASHIONABLE ACCESSORIES. The wealthy bucks of the period sported gold *buttons* on coat and waistcoat, although brass buttons were also worn by many men of fashion, including the great Beau Brummell. In 1818, the art of gilding brass buttons was generally practised. *Fobs* were much worn and consisted of two bars of gold or pinchbeck attached to a black *moiré* ribbon, the top bar having a swivel which hooked on to the watch, and the bottom bar having a ring from which one or more seals were hung. The *quizzing-glass*, or 'quizzer', of the eighteenth century was still in use, and also, of course, the indispensable *snuff-box*. A rival to the snuff-taking habit gradually appeared during this period in the form of the *cigar*. The *cigarro* was already generally popular in Spain. No doubt the habit was stimulated in England by the Anglo-Indian returning from his expeditions against Tippoo Sahib with a consignment of cheroots. Smoking gradually increased after the Battle of Waterloo.

Phosphorus matches were first made in Paris in 1805. They were very rare and regarded more as a novelty than a useful article.

WOMEN'S COSTUME

Paris still continued to be the centre of fashion in women's dress. But no longer were these fashions set by royal ladies. At the beginning of the nineteenth century this privilege belonged to the great ladies of the drama, of whom Mlle Mars was one of the most celebrated. She was born in 1779, and became the popular star of the Théâtre Français from 1799 onwards, her most successful parts being in the masterpieces of Molière. She died in 1847. Another famous lady was Signora Grassini, a beautiful Italian singer and actress, who from 1810 to 1825 had all the great men of Europe at her feet. She had, as stated by a contemporary, 'the manner of a gipsy, and dressed in splendid garments like a walking rag fair'. On the English stage a similar position was occupied by Mrs. Dorothy Jordan, who, born in 1762, made her first appearance on the stage in 1777. In 1790 she formed a connexion with William, Duke of Clarence (afterwards William IV), and all their ten children took the name of 'Fitzclarence'.

Fig. 16. Mrs. Jordan

In the intervals between her domestic duties she frequently returned to the stage. She died in 1816. Fig. 16 shows her in the fashionable dress she wore in *Matrimony*.

Actresses and *prime donne*, while creating their various roles, also created 'la Mode' with the dresses and historical costumes which they wore. During the first twenty-five or thirty years of the century many features of contemporary dress were derived from period costumes worn on the stage, many of which were excruciatingly pseudo-period.

In everyday dress the French Revolution wrought as great a change in feminine as in masculine modes.

THE GRECIAN STYLE of dress came in in 1790, when the Reign of Terror abated and Robespierre, the 'King of Terror', died at the guillotine, 28th July 1794. Women of the upper classes indulged their fancy in this new style of classic dress to an extravagant degree. They did it thoroughly, abandoning all undergarments which in any way spoilt the line of clinging drapery. To be 'well-undressed' was a usual expression when describing a smart woman of this time. The Greek fashion persisted in France throughout the Directory, the Consulate, and the First Empire, and was, of course, adopted in England and Germany. Although its popularity was greatly due to the influence of the French painter David (who became famous after the year 1784), and his enthusiasm for the classic line of ancient Greece, the fashionable one-piece garment worn at this time was actually evolved from the English *chemise*. It was naturally longer and wider than the chemise, but it had a similar draw-string at the neck, and another draw-string below the breast by which it could be gathered in and draped to suit the wearer's fancy. This was the first costume for several centuries in any way approximating to the natural feminine form.

In course of time the neck-line grew considerably lower, whilst the draw-string below the breast was brought up to give a high-waisted effect. The sleeves were also shortened and sometimes dispensed with altogether. At the same time the train grew longer, and was frequently looped up by a cord hanging from the back of the shoulder. In this long-skirted form, the dress became known as the EMPIRE GOWN (see Plate IV). It was made of light, clinging gauze, or fine muslin, in strong contrast to the stiff satins and brocades in vogue prior to 1790. Some dresses, however, were made of a *glacé* silk very like taffeta. White was the favourite colour for these classic robes, although other light colours were frequently employed.

About the year 1804 a *bodice* (or *corsage*) was added, to which the dress itself was sewn. The dress maintained its width at the top and was gathered in to the bodice in large pleats or folds. The bodice was very simple in cut, as short as possible, and very low in front. It was laced up either at the back or front, the lacing being concealed beneath a fold of the material.

Fig. 17 is a drawing made from a dress of the period. It is carried out in embroidered Indian muslin with narrow insertions of lace. Fig. 18 shows further details of the cut. In A is seen the bodice and

skirt laid out flat, the oval appendage being the train.   B is a side view
of the bodice and C back view of the bodice.

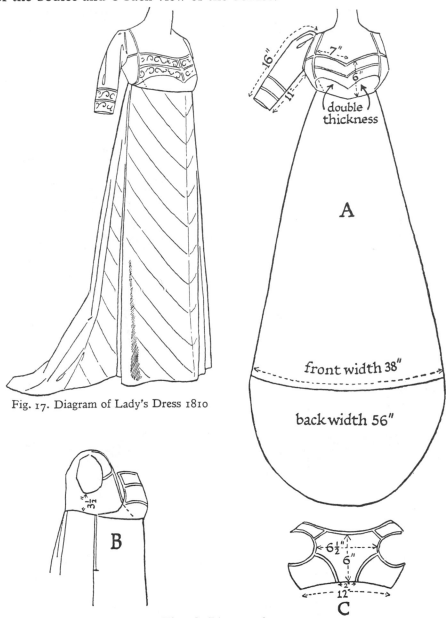

Fig. 17. Diagram of Lady's Dress 1810

double thickness

A

front width 38″

back width 56″

B

C

Fig. 18. Diagram of cut

In 1810 a fairly stiff silk called 'gros grain' and a soft silk known as
'sarcenet' were much in vogue.

TRIMMINGS. The dresses were often trimmed, very simply, with white embroidery or tinsel drawn work, chiefly at the hem and round the sleeves. Later, the front of the dress was also ornamented (see Fig. 19). From 1810 onwards, the material of the dress itself was

Fig. 19. Lady 1810   Fig. 20. Ball Dress 1816

used for trimming in the form of diagonal stripes and thin rolls. In 1816 a variety of charming trimmings in piped shapes was introduced. These often took the form of flowers or petals. Fig. 20 is taken from an actual dress of this period. It is carried out in pale blue satin veiled with Brussels net. The bodice is decorated with three tiny bands of blue piped with white, each band having three groups of points, one at each end and one in the middle. The short puff sleeves are treated in the same manner, but on the skirt there are two rows of double petals piped with white, the bottom row being in a deeper tone of blue than the upper.   The high coronal of roses shown in the

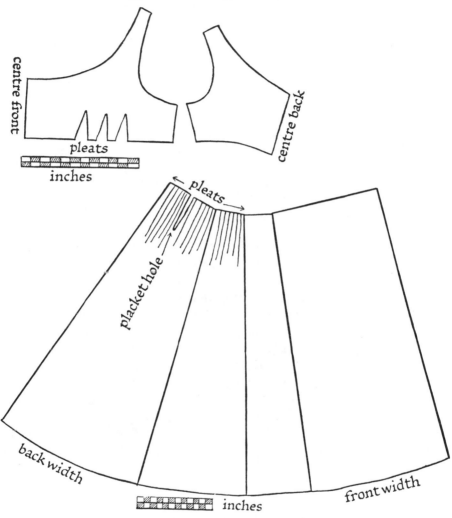

Fig. 21. Diagram of cut

figure is a very fashionable head ornament of the year 1816.   Fig. 21 shows the cut of the skirt and the half front and half back of the bodice. Fig. 22 gives the alternative cut of a short-waisted bodice of this period.

In addition to the trimmings already mentioned, drawn tulle was frequently employed, also floral designs in piped material decorated with beads or pearls.   Towards 1820, a good deal of coarse work in heavy gold tinsel was seen, as well as a variety of delicate designs in fine gold thread.

THE BODICE AND DRESS. After 1812, high-necked bodices came in again, the wide low-necked style being usually worn only at dances or on other ceremonial occasions.

The introduction of the bodice affected the form of the dress, which

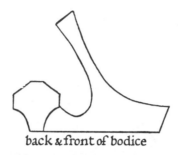

back & front of bodice

Fig. 22. Alternative cut of Bodice

was now made with fewer folds. By 1807, dresses were so close-fitting that it was nearly impossible to walk in them, and the outlines of the figure were clearly revealed. Fashion decreed that only one very thin *petticoat* should be worn, and even this was often omitted.

In 'English Costume from Pocket-Books' (1799) an amusing story is told of a Russian officer who, accustomed in his own country to estimating a lady's rank from the warmth of her clothing, offered a woman of fashion in Bond Street a penny, under the impression that from her nakedness she must be a pauper. It is also related that ladies at this period went so far as to soak their dresses in water immediately before putting them on, so that they might cling more closely to the figure. One wonders whether the death-rate from pneumonia was proportionately high. At any rate consumption, or 'decline' as it was called, was considered extremely modish and many 'Society' ladies affected this complaint. Fainting at the right moment, and fits of hysterics at every conceivable opportunity, were arts studied by every fine lady no matter what her age.

These tight dresses without folds, called '*robes en caleçon*', remained fashionable until about 1820. It must not be imagined, however, that all the garments of this period were of a diaphanous nature. The dress shown in Fig. 23 is draped in a more elaborate manner of pseudo-classic type. Several heavier dresses of a plain cut, mostly in velvet and silk, were worn about 1810–12. It should be noted also that from 1810 onwards dresses began to be worn shorter again (see Plate V).

The following excerpt from a letter dated August 1814 gives the English opinion of French fashions.

The women's dress is affectedly simple—white muslin, very short waists, very full petticoats; but the ugliest part of their habiliments is the high chimneys on

Fig. 23. Outdoor Dress 1800

their hats, which chimneys are covered with feathers and flowers. I ventured to express my dislike of the high chimney bonnets, but all the gentlemen defended them, as well as the ladies.

The quantities of rouge the Parisian ladies wear is to an English eye very disagreeable. The Tournure [1] of their throat and person is, with few exceptions, extremely elegant, and said to be greatly improved since the Revolution, by the disuse of stays, and by other contrivances which have succeeded them.

[1] This word was afterwards applied to the Bustle, see Chapter VI, page 208.

It is recorded in this year, 1814, that the Princess of Wales appeared in a MORNING DRESS of 'crimson velvet up to the throat, looking very well'. Her Royal Highness's portrait in the National Portrait Gallery,

Fig. 24. Caroline Princess of Wales 1817

London, shows her wearing this dress. At a ball given at Geneva on 16th August 1814, in honour of the Princess of Wales, her lady-in-waiting, Lady Charlotte Bury, relates that she caused a sensation by appearing 'dressed *en Vénus*, or rather not dressed, further than the waist. I was, as she used to say herself, "all over shock". A more injudicious choice of costume could not be adopted. She waltzed the

whole night, with pertinacious obstinacy'. In 1807 the Waltz was introduced into England via France and Germany.   It was considered very
improper and 'calculated to lead to the most licentious consequences'.

Fig. 25. Riding Habit 1817

About 1817 a revival of the Quadrille became the mode.   Mr. Duval,
a teacher of dancing, advertises in this year that he 'teaches the
Quadrilles in the most fashionable style of grace and elegance, as they
are now danced in London, Bath, Paris, etc.'

The Princess of Wales is shown in Fig. 24 in a simple WALKING

DRESS with a taffeta PELISSE, the chief features of which are the upstanding collar and raised epaulettes. Round the neck she wears the fashionable FRAISE, a neck-ruff composed of pleated lace or goffered lawn generally in two or three tiers. The headdress consists of the indoor cap with ruched edgings fastened under the chin and over it a rather large crowned straw hat with brim of varying width coquettishly turned off the face on one side and decorated with a large cluster of ostrich plumes. A large fur muff completes the ensemble.

The silver BRIDAL DRESS of Princess Charlotte (daughter of George, Prince of Wales and Princess Caroline), worn on her marriage in 1816, is to be seen in the London Museum.

Fig. 25 is an illustration of the *Glengarry* RIDING HABIT, an interesting fashion of the year 1817. 'It is composed of the finest pale blue cloth, and richly ornamented with frogs and braiding to correspond. The front, which is braided on each side, fastens under the body of the habit, which slopes down on each side in a very novel style, and in such a manner as to define the figure to considerable advantage. The epaulettes and jacket are braided to correspond with the front, as is also the bottom of the sleeve, which is braided nearly half way up the arm. The habit-shirt is composed of cambric, with a high standing collar, trimmed with lace. The cravat is of soft muslin, richly worked at the ends and tied in a full bow, and there are narrow lace ruffles at the wrists. The headdress takes the form of a Glengarry cap, composed of blue satin, and trimmed with plaited ribbon of various shades of blue, and a superb plume of feathers. Blue kid gloves are worn and half-boots.' We are informed that this riding-habit was designed by a dress-maker named Miss M'Donald, who was presumably inspired by feelings of extreme patriotism.

A fashionable *walking dress* of about 1820 is illustrated in Plate VI carried out in Pompeian red (a modish hue) decorated with plaitings on the bodice and wrists, petals on the shoulder puffs and ruchings at the bottom of the skirt, all these trimmings being of the same material as the dress itself. With it is worn a TIPPET of green satin. The bonnet is covered with the same material as the dress and trimmed with bands and bows of silk in the same shade of green. The RETICULE matches the dress.

The reappearance of the bodice in 1803 was accompanied by *over-dresses* wrapped over in front in the Greek style (see Fig. 26). These garments, sometimes called *tunics*, were generally cut in the same way as the dress, but were sometimes open in front. Napoleon I made the open tunic a necessary part of Court dress. In France it was often called the 'robe turque' or 'robe à la prêtresse'.

About 1810, these robes disappeared in their tunic form, having gradually developed into new articles of apparel known as *redingotes*. These were in use for morning wear or to take the place of cloaks in cold weather. They were generally high at the neck, with long close-

Fig. 26. Classic Evening Dress 1804   Fig. 27. Redingote 1814

fitting sleeves. From 1812 onwards, they were often made with a broad collar of coloured material and rather full gathered sleeves (see Fig. 27).

Another quaint form of overdress worn during the first ten years of the nineteenth century was the *robe en tablier*, an overapron with sleeves made to fasten at the back with a few ribbon bows or buttons. This garment varied in length, sometimes reaching a little above the knees, sometimes being as long as the dress worn beneath.

Yet another innovation was the *Spencer*, a short jacket with long

Fig. 28. Pelisse 1815   Fig. 29. Pelisse 1819

sleeves worn over the dress, closely resembling the bodice of a high-necked dress. In colour and material it generally differed from the dress worn with it (see Plate V). The cut of this garment is very similar to that of the bodice shown in diagram, Fig. 17. This style of jacket was very popular from 1800 to 1830. Several charming examples are to be seen in the Victoria and Albert Museum.

In addition to the redingotes and spencers, the *pelisse* was an outer garment considerably worn at this time. Fig. 28 shows a pelisse of 1815, and Fig. 29 one of 1819.

SLEEVES. Short sleeves disappeared about 1812, and the long sleeves which succeeded them were constantly varied. The style most favoured was a gathered sleeve drawn tight in several places (see Fig. 27). The spencer jacket or bodice was sometimes made with a short puff sleeve worn over a fairly loose long sleeve gathered in at the wrist. With the short sleeves, long *gloves* or *mittens* were often worn (see Figs. 23 and 26).

COURT DRESS. A very important subject in the history of costume is Court dress.

In the early part of the reign of George III the hoop and, later, the panier was worn for Court, as well as for full dress and smart wear. To this was added a train of varying amplitude falling from the back of the waist. A low neck, elbow sleeves, and powdered coiffure surmounted with ostrich plumes completed this toilet. Such was the ceremonial costume worn at the Courts of Queen Marie Antoinette and Queen Charlotte.

Hoops and *paniers* disappeared from among the fashionable for everyday and full dress in England in the early seventeen-eighties, but were retained for full Court dress until 1820. The Revolution of 1787 banished it entirely from France.

The hoop had a very ungainly appearance when disassociated from a long, tapering waist, and especially was this the case when worn with the short waist fashionable during the first twenty years of the nineteenth century. For this reason the hoop was not revived at the Imperial French Court.

Fig. 30 shows the type of ceremonial dress worn at the Court of Josephine from 1804 to the end of the First Empire. The robe is cut on the fashionable high-waisted lines, and carried out in white satin heavily embroidered in silver at the hem, which is finished by a border of silver fringe. The perpendicular lines of embroidery are very characteristic of the period. The sleeves are composed of pointed lace, and similar lace frills decorate the shoulders. The long, narrow Court train of green velvet, embroidered in silver and lined with white satin, is fastened round the high waist by a narrow silver strap secured with a jewelled ornament. The hair is dressed 'à la grecque' and, embellished with a classic diadem of diamonds, several ostrich plumes and a gauze veil.

It may be mentioned that the dressmaker to the Court of Napoleon

was the celebrated M. Leroi, who personally costumed the Empress
Joséphine.   He was the rival of, and eventually successor to, the famous
Rose Bertin, who had been Court dressmaker to Marie Antoinette,
and who lived until 1813.

Fig. 31 illustrates a full dress worn at the Court of St. James's during
the Regency.   It is composed of a foundation of pale pink satin, veiled
with a robe of white gauze elaborately embroidered and decorated with
lace, and a short, draped overdress of the same material.   Posies of

Fig. 30. Court Dress, French Empire

pink peonies are strewn over the garment with studied negligence, and there is a single peony on each shoulder. It will be noted that the dress has the very fashionable high waist of the period, worn with a hoop. The skirt of this Court dress is ankle-length and worn without a train. The sleeves are barely more than shoulder-straps edged with ruched lace, and the same ruching decorates the décolletage. The loose girdle, worn below the waist-line, is completed with tassels. The hair is dressed rather high, with the usual classical curls at the side of the face, and confined by a narrow, jewelled coronet. Ruched lace lappets hanging at the back and numerous ostrich-plumes rising from the coronet complete the headdress.

Fig. 32 is an example of a French Court dress of 1818 (during the reign of Louis XVIII). The dress is carried out in white satin with a flounce of white lace. The rows of padded satin (or 'rouleau') which appear on the bodice, sleeves, and skirt are very characteristic. These rouleaux are bound at intervals with a silver cord. The train, which is attached round the high waist, is of rose-coloured velvet decorated with a border of white silk roses and green leaves. A noticeable feature of this Court costume is the band of lace worn over the high hairdressing to which long lace lappets are attached.

The following Order for COURT MOURNING, issued by the Lord Chamberlain's Office, St. James's Palace, 19th November 1818, 'for her late Majesty the Queen, of blessed memory', is of interest:

The Ladies to wear black bombazines, plain muslins or long lawn linen, crape hoods, shamoy [1] shoes and gloves, and crape fans.
Undress—Dark Norwich crape.
The Gentlemen to wear black cloth, without buttons on the sleeves and pockets, plain muslin or long lawn cravats and weepers, shamoy shoes and gloves, crape hat bands and black swords and buckles.
Undress—Dark grey frocks.

'Bombazine' was spun from wefts of fine Norfolk and Kent wool, the worsted being thrown upon the right side. For a long period it was only used in black, and for mourning purposes, but was afterwards sold in colours.

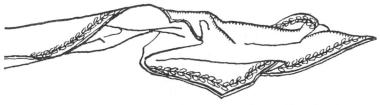

<hr />

1 'Shamoy' is, of course, a period spelling for chamois.

UNDERCLOTHES. Although an excessively thin petticoat was practically the only undergarment worn, it must not be forgotten that the Empress

Fig. 31. Court Dress, English 1810

Josephine first introduced white washable underclothes into France at the beginning of the nineteenth century. In fact this imperial lady changed her linen (what little of it she wore) three times a day. Her husband, probably from economic reasons, had only one shirt per diem.

This period is also noteworthy for the complete absence of stays, fashion demanding that the natural figure should be untrammelled. With the extremely classic type of dress the *outrée* woman of fashion left her legs bare beneath the filmy robe.   Others compromised by wearing

Fig. 32. Court Dress, French 1818

long flesh-coloured or delicately tinted stockings equivalent to modern tights.

WRAPS. In addition to the overdresses and spencers previously described, a great variety of *wraps* and *shawls* were in use.   About 1800, large rectangular shawls, worn like a Greek Chlamys, were very fashionable.   For these the favourite materials were muslin, crape, or Norwich silk in white or some other light colour.   *Oriental cashmere shawls* were also much worn (see Plate IV). The fashion appeared in England in the year 1786, its popularity among all well-dressed women, which lasted many years, was due to the fact that its draping, manner of wearing, and manipulation demanded great personal skill. Hence the fashionable expression was to be 'well draped', or 'beautifully draped'. The cashmere shawl measured at the time of its introduction six yards by two yards,[1] and cost anything from twenty to fifty pounds. For the less wealthy, shawls were produced in printed cotton.

In 1814 the V-shaped BERTHE made its first appearance, though it did not really become established until the thirties. Other features during the first twenty years of the century were lace and embroidered *fichus*, long *scarf-capes*, and a simple *pelisse*, with or without a cape. About 1810, however, all these wraps suffered in popularity from the introduction of the *redingote*, of which mention has already been made. Although not strictly *à la mode*, *cloaks* of miscellaneous style were frequently worn in winter. In 1808 fur cloaks were worn by fashionable women of Paris.

COLLARS AND NECKWEAR. In 1803 the neck and bosom were sometimes hidden under a lace or linen CHEMISETTE which came up to the neck, terminating in a tiny stand-up collar. A high *Vandyke lace collar* with a fan setting to shoulders also appeared. Collars of this type were called BETSIES and were said to be an imitation of the ruffs worn by Queen Elizabeth. But, generally speaking, the fashion prevailed of leaving the neck and shoulders uncovered. After 1815 embroidered ruffles and frills decorated most of the high-necked bodices (see Fig. 28, and Plate VI).

FURS in various styles were worn in winter, the fur being used as a lining to dark-hued velvet or heavy silk. In cold weather the spencer jacket was often lined with fur. Large size MUFFS were also popular (see Fig. 29).

FOOTWEAR. High-heeled shoes were abolished after the French Revolution. Throughout the whole of the early nineteenth century shoes with flat heels were worn. The shoe was at first pointed and tied like a sandal up the leg to carry out the Grecian style in vogue. About 1810, a shoe with rounded toe, tied in the same manner, became fashionable. From 1808 low boots, ankle high, were sometimes seen.

HEADDRESSES. During this period there was a singular variety of hats, bonnets, and turbans. Several cockade hats and top-hats of masculine form were worn during the latter part of George III's reign. Bonnets grew gradually smaller, and by 1815 were generally close

---

[1] The same dimensions as the Greek Himation. See Vol. I, p. 44.

fitting. A frequent variation was a handkerchief tied over the top of a straw hat and secured beneath the chin, termed 'the Gipsy hat'. Hats and bonnets were decorated with large ribbon bows, ruchings, flowers, or ostrich feathers. The materials mostly used for covering hats were satin, plush, and velvet. Several pleasing examples of bonnets are to be found in 'Bell's Fashionable Magazine', 1812. (One of these is shown in Plate VI.)

Hats and bonnets constructed in straw, felt, silk, gauze, etc., on the lines of classic helmets were much in vogue. '*Casquets à l'Athène*' and '*Casquets à la Minerve*' are among the fancy names given to these headdresses (see Fig. 33). Medieval tilting helmets of black velvet or silver tissue surmounted by coloured ostrich feathers followed those of

Fig. 33. Casquet à l'Athène   Fig. 34. Tilting Casquet

Classic style (see Fig. 34) and these, in their turn, developed into the coal-scuttle bonnet which held its own for half a century.

'*Spanish*' hats, consisting of a moderate sized crown with a wide turned-up brim in front, were also worn and were decorated with a sweeping ostrich plume. One for the year 1804 is described as of 'Brown Egyptian earth colour velvet with a white ostrich feather'. Another somewhat on the lines of a sombrero was of 'purple velvet turned up in front and ornamented with feathers of the same colour'.

The *turban*, as distinct from the 'Pouf' of an earlier date, was much worn in England after 1792 and was inspired by the military operations then being carried out in India. A little later turbans became fashionable in France as the result of Napoleon's Egyptian campaign (1798). A '*turban à la Mameluk*' had an inverted flower-pot or fez of gold tissue surrounded by a full puffing of white satin. In front of this was set a gold and ruby crescent, and a white ostrich feather fell over the left side.

Military hats, stimulated by the warlike times, were carried out in velvet, silk, felt, gauze or other materials to represent the helmets worn by the officers in Napoleon's army. One given in a fashion plate of the time has a large semi-spherical headpiece and roll brim of 'light blue beaver, covered with light blue netting ornamented with a white feather'. It has the appearance of the headgear worn by a dragoon (see Fig. 35).

HAIRDRESSING. The use of powder for the hair had gone out at the end of the French Revolution. In 1800 the hair was generally gathered into a knot of curls rather high up at the back of the head, with a side curl in front by each ear. After 1808, the side curls were elaborated and known as '*tire-buchons*', several being arranged on either cheek.

Fig. 35. Military Casquet

Sometimes the Grecian mode was adopted with a curled fringe on the forehead, one or more fillets bound across the head, and a mass of pendant curls at the back (see Plate V).

Women also freely borrowed from masculine styles, the '*coiffure à la Titus*' being specially popular. This was acquired by 'cutting the hair close to the root, in order to give each hair its natural stiffness which makes it grow perpendicularly'. Merveilleuses and Muscadins were frequently barbered '*à la Titus*', all shorn, and with some long locks in disorder on the forehead. Shingling of 1923 was not so original after all!

In 1812 a simplified style of hairdressing was much in vogue, the hair being parted in the middle, combed smoothly towards the sides, and curled, whilst the back hair was arranged in a simple coil. For evening wear some sort of headdress was usual, either in the form of a *turban* or a scarf bound round the head and embellished with an ostrich plume (see Plate IV).

BAGS AND PURSES. Up to 1820 the long stocking-purse was often tucked through the belt or waistband. It was set with a pair of metal rings and had also steel or gilt beaded tassels. Large and small circular purses made in coloured silk threads were also in use, as well as the plain money-bag with a draw-string. Reticules or vanity bags of the Empire Period were made of cardboard, leather, or tin, covered with material embroidered or painted to represent Greek vases or amphorae. They were often spoken of at the time as 'ridicules'.

PARASOLS were of varied design, some flat, others with round or pagoda-shaped tops, but all kinds were of a small size. At the beginning of this period the stick was jointed and hinged so that it could be folded up and held in the hand when the parasol was closed. It also had a contrivance which enabled the top part, when open, to be set at an angle. Rings were sometimes attached to the ferrule and threaded with a loop of ribbon and bow by which means it was often carried. Fringe began to make its appearance at the edge of the shade.

The *Umbrella* or *Parapluie* was of larger size and when closed had a somewhat bulky appearance. The stick was of normal length. Umbrellas were also used by gentlemen.

FANS with ivory sticks, semicircular and made to close, were small, measuring not more than six inches when closed.

MUCH JEWELLERY was worn as a relief to the very simple dresses in vogue during the Empire Period. Necklaces, earrings, bracelets, rings on the fingers and rings on the toes—if the ultra fashionable were shod in sandals—anklets, combs, and diadems, fashioned after the Greek Stephane were all worn for full dress. These were made by the gold-smiths of the time after Greek models. The most exotic purchased collections of antiques for personal use.

An amusing story, with reference to jewellery, was told at this time:

A noble Lord once applied to a pawnbroker to lend him a thousand guineas on his wife's diamonds, for which he had paid four thousand. 'Take the articles to pieces,' said his lordship, 'number the stones, and put false ones in their place, my lady will not distinguish them.' 'You are too late, my lord,' said the pawnbroker, 'your lady has gained a march upon you, for these stones are false, having bought the diamonds of her Ladyship last year.'

LIST OF ARTISTS WORKING DURING THIS REIGN

'Francisco José Goya y Lucientes'	1745–1828
Jacques Louis David	1748–1825
Henry Raeburn	1756–1823
Thomas Rowlandson	1756–1827
James Gillray	1757–1815
François Pascal Gérard	1770–1837
Alfred Edward Chalon	1780–1860
Jean Auguste Dominique Ingres	1780–1867

CHAPTER II

REIGN OF GEORGE IV (1820–30)

CONTEMPORARY FOREIGN GOVERNMENTS

FRANCE: Louis XVIII (1814–24)
Charles X (1824–30)
PRUSSIA: Frederick William III (1797–1840)
AUSTRIA: Francis I (1804–35)
RUSSIA: Alexander I (1801–25)
Nicholas I (1825–55)
SPAIN: Ferdinand VII (1814–33)
ITALY: Various Independent Governments

INTRODUCTION

GEORGE IV was born on 12th August 1762; on 8th April 1795 he married Caroline Amelia Elizabeth of Brunswick-Wolfenbüttel (who died 7th August 1821). Their only child was Charlotte Augusta, born 7th March 1796. This princess married, 2nd May 1816, Leopold, reigning Duke of Saxe-Coburg-Saalfeld, and died 6th November 1817.

On 29th January 1820, George III departed this life, and, at long last, the Prince Regent, who had understudied his father for so many years, found himself in the principal role; and, as monarch of Great Britain and Ireland, was able to give full reign to his flamboyant and romantic tendencies.

It is doubtful if any of our 'dressy kings' have evinced more interest in the garments they wore than George IV; a reputation for being 'well-dressed' was a sure passport to the royal favour, especially if the candidate, by that judicious imitation which is the surest flattery, subscribed to the popular idea that His Majesty was the 'last word' in the realm of fashion.

His coronation in July 1821 was an occasion of which George IV took full sartorial advantage, and, despite the sneering references to 'the puppet show which cost half a million', its pomp and magnificence had not been equalled since 'The Field of the Cloth of Gold'. The King's royal robes alone cost twenty-four thousand pounds. The official

38

account of King George IV's coronation was entrusted to Sir George Naylor, and was illustrated by engravings of pictures by P. Stephanoff.

Fig. 36. King George IV

A year later Sir Thomas Lawrence (1769–1830), writing to his sister, 1st July 1822, says:

I was never in more urgent occupations than at this moment, when I am completing, with other pictures, a portrait of the King in his private dress—perhaps my most successful resemblance of him, and the most interesting from its being so entirely of a simple domestic character.

The portrait to which he refers, showing the King seated, is now in the Wallace Collection (No. 559), and Fig. 36 is drawn from it.

For this portrait the King wears a skirted coat made of fine black cloth, single-breasted. The roll collar is of sable, and the same fur descends on the left side of the coat. It is lined with black satin and is fastened with elaborate frogging (see detail), with more braiding on the left side than on the right. The sleeves, normal on the shoulders, are moderately close fitting, and come well on to the wrists, showing a small amount of white shirt-cuff. The knee-breeches are of black silk, and worn with fine black silk stockings and black varnished low shoes having small black bows. The coiffure is '*à la Brutus*'. A black top-hat and pale yellow gloves are carried. His Majesty wears the Golden Fleece suspended from a broad red ribbon below his black satin stock, and the Star of the Garter on his breast, and it would appear that these two Orders were habitually worn by His Majesty in everyday attire.

The minutest detail complementary to the fashionable attire of the period was carefully observed by the King. Although—unlike his mother—he was not partial to snuff, custom ordained that snuff should be *de rigueur* for the exquisite of the day, and accordingly His Majesty invariably carried a snuff-box; therefrom he would ostentatiously extract his pinch of the aromatic powder, which he would convey 'twixt right thumb and forefinger to the Royal nostrils, but was careful to drop it *unostentatiously*, before it reached them.

Even the prerogative of royalty did not render the King's taste in dress —possibly a trifle exotic, not to say bizarre—immune from somewhat acid criticism. Sir Morgan O'Doherty, Bart., once wrote that George IV might have had a great many good points about him—concocting punch was one!—

but as to dressing, he had the vilest taste. I remember seeing him one day in a purple velvet waistcoat, with a running stripe of a gold tree, surmounted with gold monkeys upon it; and congratulating him on his exquisite taste in the selection of colours, he felt evidently very proud of my approbation, but when I recommended him a yellow coat with purple braiding, I think he smelt a rat—he did not ask me to Carlton House [1] for nearly a month afterwards.

After his coronation the King paid visits to Ireland and to his kingdom in Hanover, and in August 1822 paid a state visit to Scotland, this being the first occasion that Scotland had been so honoured since the days of the Stuarts. In earlier days the King, then Prince of Wales, had shown considerable sympathy with the House of Stuart, and had paid a visit to Henry Stuart, Cardinal York, in Rome. Later, the cardinal bequeathed to the Prince Regent the crown jewels of Great

[1] Carlton House, familiarly known as 'Nero's Hotel'.

Britain, which his grandfather, King James II, had carried away with him to France in 1688.

Whatever may have been the prince's feelings with regard to the Act of Settlement of 1701, the death of Cardinal York, the last of the Stuarts, in 1807, removed all ideas of usurpation.

The King embarked for the north at Greenwich, whither he travelled in a plain royal carriage, escorted by a party of hussars. 'He wore a blue coat and FORAGING CAP (see Fig. 37), his trousers were

Fig. 37. Forage Cap

white, and his boots were *à la Wellington.*' 'When His Majesty landed on the spot sacred to the tread of royalty . . . he wore the full-dress uniform of an admiral; with St. Andrew's Cross, and a large thistle in his gold-laced hat. . . . The King mounted his carriage, while cavalry and Highland Infantry, and the Gentlemen Archers of the Royal Guard, saluted him in the due forms of their respective services', and so he entered Edinburgh!

Sir Walter Scott was much to the fore during King George's Scottish visit and Sir David Wilkie composed a dramatic, not to say theatrical, picture showing George IV, aged sixty, looking extremely youthful and elegant in his Guard's uniform and wearing the full insignia of the Most Noble Order of the Garter, receiving the keys of Holyrood Palace. The King is surrounded by officials and courtiers, many of them in Highland dress.

The following day a levee was held in the long gallery of Holyrood Palace; it is noteworthy that the previous levee held at Holyrood had been that to which Prince Charles had summoned his adherents seventy-seven years before. The Scottish nobility attended in full force, and as a graceful compliment to the national feeling 'The King wore the Highland costume, selecting the tartan of the Stuarts as the colour of his dress'.

The following, taken from a local contemporary newspaper, gives interesting details of the costume worn at that function.

On this occasion no gentleman can appear otherwise than in a full-dress suit, with sword and bag; but hair powder is not now held to be indispensable.   Gentlemen may appear in any uniform to which they have a right, and for those who present themselves as Highlanders, the ancient costume of their country is always sufficient dress.   Those who wear the Highland dress must, however, be careful to be armed in the proper Highland fashion—steel-wrought pistols, broadsword and dirk.   It is understood that Glengarry, Breadalbane, Huntly, and several other chieftains mean to attend the levee, 'with their tail on', i.e. with a considerable attendance of their gentlemen followers.

The minute description of the revival of national Highland costume is indeed interesting in view of the fact that after the rebellion of 1745 the wearing of Highland dress was prohibited by the Act of 1747.   The picturesque costume worn early in the nineteenth century may be studied in the works of Sir Thomas Lawrence; 'The Cock of the North' by George Sanders; and the portrait of Sir John Sinclair by Sir Henry Raeburn, etc., etc.

Amongst other famous Scotsmen at the levee was the Laird of Macnab in the gorgeous and barbaric panoply of full Highland dress. It is said that he entered the Royal presence wearing his feathered bonnet, and advanced towards the King with a grand and haughty air, befitting one whose ancestors had bulked so largely in the history of Scotland since the beginning of time.   His sovereign was so amazed at the magnificent appearance of the Scottish nobleman, that he conceived the idea of commanding Sir Henry Raeburn to paint a portrait of 'The Macnab'.   This well-known picture used to hang in Holyrood House, but in 1911 it was in the possession of the Hon. Mrs. Baillie Hamilton; it was, later, purchased by Messrs. Dewar, and so has become familiar to all modern consumers of whisky.

The 'Edinburgh Star' also relates:

Since the period when James VI left Scotland to assume the sceptre of the United Kingdom, Edinburgh has not been visited by any Sovereign in the full and undisturbed enjoyment of regal splendour and power.   Charles II is the only king who has ever seen it.

No wonder such a fuss was made over so auspicious an event!

But advancing old-age, ill-health, or possibly a surfeit of the life of pleasure in which he had indulged for so many years, brought a sudden end to the evanescent splendour in which the reign of 'George the Magnificent' had opened.   The King withdrew from Society, and except for essential appearances at state functions shut himself up in 'The Cottage' at Windsor, or in his beloved Pavilion at Brighton.   He developed into a peevish, whimsical, thoroughly selfish recluse, with failing health and few friends.   A startling exception was made on the occasion of the visit to England of the Portuguese Dom Miguel, for whom the King once again blossomed forth in his pristine splendour.

Even in his retirement, and in spite of the fact that the Royal leadership in clothes was more or less a thing of the past, we know that His Majesty remained somewhat spruce in dress.   We are also informed that the Court tailor, Mr. Cobham of Windsor, used to go up to the castle every evening to see to the buttons and buttonholes of the garments which the King had worn during the day.   Mr. Cobham's job was probably no sinecure, as the King's predilection for skin-tight garments must, of necessity, have put a severe strain on the Royal fastenings.

Like many earlier crowned heads of England this king had a mania for hoarding clothes, and at his death on the 26th June 1830 all the garments that had ever graced his august person during the course of fifty years were found in his wardrobes.   These were sold for £15,000. They must have cost ten times as much!

The Age of Romanticism, which was in full swing during this reign, had its origin in France among the opulent citizen class in the last decade, approximately with the accession of Louis XVIII.   It was a reaction from Classic Culture to Medieval Romance, greatly stimulated by the writings of Victor Hugo (b. 1802, first work 1822, d. 1885), Alexandre Dumas (Père) (b. 1803, first work 1826, d. 1870), and our own Sir Walter Scott (b. 1771, first work 1804, d. 1832).

John Nash, the celebrated architect, was born in London in 1752. He came into prominence in 1792 and in 1815 promoted and planned improvements in the West End of London.   His most important works were Regent Street and Buckingham Palace.   He was also the architect of the Pavilion at Brighton.   He died in 1835.

MEN'S COSTUME

The Masculine World of Fashion at this time was centred in London.

Among the Exquisites of this reign must be mentioned Charles, Viscount Petersham, later fourth Earl of Harrington.   Born in 1780, in early life he was attached to the Court and was Lord of the Bedchamber to George III and George IV.   This versatile nobleman had many faculties.   He was a connoisseur of tea and snuff, and spent much time in perfecting a receipt for boot-blacking.   As an inventor he was celebrated for his concoction of a snuff mixture; his own personal supply, being sold by auction at his death in 1851, realized £3,000.

His collection of snuff-boxes was the finest in England, as he possessed a sufficient number to enable him to use a different one every day of the year. Even his liveries, his carriages and horse-furniture were of snuff colour. His lordship was also the inventor of an overcoat and breeches which were made of a special heavy woollen cloth with a round nap surface. It is recorded he wore these garments in sky-blue, and both overcoat and cloth received the name of the inventor—'Petersham'. Ribbon was not in his line, nevertheless a thick ribbon used chiefly as belting was honoured with his name.

Coats and Overcoats. Soon after 1820, both the *dress coat* and the *overcoat* were made in a different fashion. Although following the lines of the diagram shown in Fig. 5, the tails were cut separately and sewn on to the body of the coat, thus ensuring a better fit. Similarly, the front lapels were cut separately from the collar, which was now nearly high enough to reach the head. Often they were very thick and stiff, and to ensure that the collar set well, and that the lapels lay neatly on the chest, the two were only partly joined, the space between taking the shape of a $<$ and later an Σ. Both collar and lapels were stiffened with an inside padding, and the coat itself was padded at breast and hips, giving a much more tight-fitting effect at the waist.

All fashionable men had slender waists. To achieve this modish effect CORSETS, made on the same principle as women's, were worn. The coat was cut to follow the graceful tapering lines, whether worn open or closed. Gentlemen with more rotund figures buttoned their coats tight to straining-point. George IV was not behind with these fashionable foibles.

Coats were generally double-breasted (see Fig. 38). The collar and lapels were sometimes of velvet, in contrast to the cloth of which the coat itself was made (see Plate VII). The vogue for sky-blue coats (see Chapter I, p. 10) continued during the whole course of this reign. George IV wore one at a levee he held during his visit to Dublin; his choice of this garment showed his lack of affection and respect for the memory of his wife, who had died only eleven days previously.

The colours most favoured for overcoats were green, grey, blue, and buff. Besides these coats, there was also the *riding coat*, which had broader tails than the dress-coat and pockets with broad flaps set in front at an angle. Charles, second Earl Grey, is mentioned as having worn in 1827 *the new overcoat called 'the Wellington'*.

About 1827, a short type of coat with single roll collar was sometimes worn. *Sleeves* were still full at the shoulder, tightening on the forearm down to the wrist, where they curved out over the hand. They were buttoned at the side.

WAISTCOATS were often double-breasted and tight at the waist, which was set fairly high. The erect collar which had been so much

Fig. 38. Gentleman 1825

in vogue at the beginning of the century became gradually narrower, until in 1820 it was merely the top end of the waistcoat folded down. From then onwards, the waistcoat usually had a round-shaped lapel and a long opening displaying the frilled shirt-front. For diagram of cut see Fig. 39. There were also waistcoats having no lapels or pockets whatever. It was still the mode to have a fob of gold seals attached to the watch inside the breeches pocket and hanging below the waistcoat (see Plate VII).

NECKWEAR. As in the preceding reign, plain black or white stocks tied with a front bow were generally worn, with or without the points of the collar showing, and a frilled or goffered shirt (see Figs. 15 and 41). According to H. Le Blanc, who published his 'Art of Tying the Cravat'

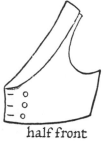

half front

Fig. 39. Diagram of Waistcoat

in 1828, there were thirty-two different styles of *cravat*. The cravat might be plain or coloured, the all-important thing was the form. This connoisseur of neckwear particularly favoured the style known as the '*Nœud Gordien*' (or Gordian Knot), but he also recognized the '*Cravate à la Byron*' (somewhat loose and flowing) and the '*Cravate Sentimentale*' (which 'may be worn from the age of seventeen to twenty-seven, but after that age cannot with propriety be patronized even by the most agreeable'). In 1828 cravats of black silk or satin were the general wear, although occasionally coloured silk handkerchiefs were swathed round the neck.

Coloured cravats were made of very costly materials, but these

can be admitted only as undress costume. The white cravat, with spots or squares is received as half-dress, but the plain white is allowed at balls or soirées. The black stock, or cravat, is only suited to military men, not on service, who are dressed in plain clothes. As to coloured cravats, they are entirely prohibited in evening parties. '*The Cravate de Bal*', when carefully put on is delightfully elegant; it partakes of the elegant *séverité* of the *Mathématique*, combined with the *laissez-aller* of the *Bergami*, whilst it unites the advantages of both. It is in fact, a derivation from them. We must here enter an entire prohibition against colour of every kind for the *Cravate de Bal*—white must reign alone. The Cravat should be but slightly starched.

The '*Cravate Mathématique*' is a combination of symmetry and regularity, all the folds in a horizontal direction forming the two acute and opposite angles of a triangle which the *Mathématique* must always strictly represent. The '*Cravate à la Bergami*' was somewhat similar to the *Cravate à la Byron*.

CLOAKS remained in fashion during this period, and were worn both with and without sleeves. Fig. 40 depicts an average well-dressed

Frenchman of the period wearing a capacious cloak. The style of cape which had obtained in the eighteenth century was still the model, but a second large cape to cover shoulders, breast, and back was some-

Fig. 40. M. Leblanc 1823   Fig. 41. Cloak 1828

times added. Cloak-capes were often trimmed with fur (see Fig. 41). The cloak was fastened in front by broad strips of cloth, those on one side holding the buttons and the others holding the button-holes. This mode of fastening remained until 1830, when the cloak was merely thrown over the shoulders, and held together by hook and chain.

Fur cloaks were worn by gentlemen early in the reign. *'Pilgrim' cloaks* were circular, having several capes one on top of the other, and

Fig. 42. Gentleman 1829

were lined with silk. Cloaks also had capes of rich fur. Towards the end of the reign cloaks were so long that they trailed upon the ground.

BREECHES AND TROUSERS. Breeches were not so much worn as trousers, except for riding and country wear (see Fig. 42). Trousers were made of drill, cloth, nankeen, and white corduroy. *Riding-breeches* were usually of white buckskin. In 1820, trousers were sometimes worn very short, hardly reaching to the ankle. Others were long and fastened with straps beneath the boots (see Plate III). The dandy of 1820–25 wore *peg-top trousers*, very full in the upper part. For evening wear, very tight-fitting breeches were worn, sometimes to the knee, sometimes reaching just above the ankle (see Plate VII). *Knee-breeches* were the only style worn at Court (see Figs. 2 and 14). For *Court dress* of this reign see Chapter V, p. 142.

CLOTHES FOR BOYS. In 1826 a characteristic fashion for young boys was the '*Dutch Skeleton Dress*' (see Fig. 43). It consisted of a rather

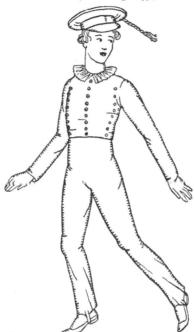

Fig. 43. Dutch Skeleton 1826

tight-fitting, high-waisted coat, with a frilled collar, and ankle-length trousers. But the distinguishing feature of the costume was the three vertical lines of buttons on the coat marking out the position of the breast-bone and ribs. An echo of this fashion may be noticed in the uniform of the modern page-boy.

FOOTWEAR. Short *Wellington boots* and shoes were chiefly worn. The *Hessian boot* with curved front and tassel was also still in use, as in the latter part of the preceding reign (see Plate I, and Fig. 12). The *top-boot* was still worn as shown in Fig. 15 and country gentlemen favoured *gaiters* (see Fig. 42). The shoes of the period were very low in the heel, with a rather round toe, and a very short tongue almost covered by small latchets.

HEADGEAR. The round hat, or top-hat, was now the order of the day, although its modifications were many (see the various drawings). In some cases the crown tapered at the top and the hat had a large curled brim (see Fig. 44); in others the crown was high and straight with a small brim, whilst yet others had a crown enlarging at the top with a small, almost straight brim. A short-crowned hat was also worn, but the cocked hat had practically disappeared. The majority of top-hats were made of beaver, but top-hats of straw were not unknown. About 1820 CAPS began to be worn, consisting of a fairly wide headpiece resembling a tam-o'-shanter gathered into a band, with a leather peak to shield the eyes. This form of cap, very often with the addition of a long tassel, was much worn by young boys of the period (see Fig. 43).

Fig. 44. Hat 1828

A type of cap worn by adults, and for semi-military duties, was known as a '*forage cap*' (previously mentioned on page 41). Fig. 37 is a drawing of a forage cap worn by George IV. The top is of blue cloth, unstiffened, having a band of gold lace about one and a half inches wide in an oak-leaf design. The black leather peak is edged with a narrow gold band and small oak-leaves. This cap was worn in rather a jaunty manner on the left side of the head.

HAIRDRESSING. The hair was still worn fairly short except on top of the head. It was very often brushed towards the front on either side, thus producing the effect of a cockscomb. The face was clean-shaven with the exception of short *side-whiskers*.

FASHIONABLE ACCESSORIES. As already mentioned, *snuff-boxes* continued to form part of a dandy's equipment, which also frequently included a quizzing-glass. *Smoking* became rather more general, and in this connection it may be mentioned that lucifer matches were first sold in 1827 at the price of one shilling and twopence per box of fifty. In view of the high price, it is not surprising that the tinder-box continued to hold its own for a considerable number of years.

Umbrellas carried by gentlemen were of the normal shape, and frequently of very large size, more than four feet in diameter.

WOMEN'S COSTUME

Women's fashions still derived their inspiration from the modes of Paris. Many of these were originated by the French actresses in conjunction with their *couturières*. The influence of the French Court was negligible, as the king (Charles X) was a widower and his immediate circle was not remarkable for its brilliance.

The first lady in France at this time was Marie Thérèse, Duchesse d'Angoulême, styled 'Madame Royale'. Born in 1778, she was the only surviving daughter of Louis XVI and Marie Antoinette. She was a woman of strong character, and Napoleon said of her that she was 'the only man in her family'. She exerted little influence in the world of fashion, as her tragic life rendered her unwilling to make frequent appearances in public. She died in 1851.

There was virtually no queen consort in England, as the king was separated from his wife, Caroline of Brunswick. Though she was sometimes referred to as Queen Caroline, her position as such was never recognized. She made an attempt to gain admittance to Westminster Abbey on the day of George IV's coronation, but was forcibly prevented from entering the building. In view of these facts, the ladies of England had no outstanding royal figure whose fashions they could imitate.

In England, one of the leaders of social elegance and culture was Margaret, Countess of Blessington. Her first husband, Captain Farmer, having died in 1817, she married in 1818 Charles John Gardiner, Earl of Blessington. The noble earl died in 1829, but Lady Blessington lived on until 1849.

Lady Caroline Lamb, another prominent leader of Society, was the daughter of William, third Earl of Bessborough, Baron Duncannon. Born in 1785, she married in 1805 Mr. William Lamb, afterwards Lord Melbourne. The authoress of several novels, she is chiefly famous for her admiration of Lord Byron. She died in 1828.

A striking feature of this period was the craze for the *Bal Masqué* and fancy dress ball which had originated about the time of Waterloo. These entertainments were increasingly popular during the first half of the nineteenth century. The subjects were historical, one given in 1829 typifying 'Marie Stuart's entry into the Tuileries'. Frequently they took their titles from Sir Walter Scott's novels. In June 1828 the grand ball of 'Queen Elizabeth at Kenilworth' was given by the Marchioness of Londonderry at Holderness House. Lady Londonderry herself represented the great queen and was surrounded by the Court 'superbly dressed in the proper costumes of the age'. Judging from contemporary engravings, they, and her ladyship's 'Elizabeth', were more 1828 than Elizabethan. The total cost of these costumes is stated to have been one hundred thousand pounds. Every one who was any one hastened to assume fancy dress. Many of these 'travestissements', as they were called, were astonishingly bizarre and *outré* versions of historical and national costume.

The stage-costumes worn by actresses at this period are of considerable interest. One of the younger players was Fanny Kemble, who, born in 1809, was the daughter of two famous artistes, Charles Kemble and Maria Theresa de Camp. Sarah Siddons, the great tragédienne, was her aunt. For her first appearance in 1829 as 'Juliet' at Covent Garden, her mother had designed for her 'a simple white satin evening gown of modern style', feeling that the young actress would be more at home in 'usual' clothes. Her dark hair was dressed high, and she wore elbow-length white gloves (see Fig. 45, taken from a contemporary print). Despite this somewhat unsuitable costume, her 'Juliet' was an instantaneous success. Before Fanny Kemble appeared as 'Euphrasia' in Murphy's *Grecian Daughter* (1829), Sir Thomas Lawrence persuaded her mother that Fanny's costumes should suit the period of the play. The result, however, was by no means purely classic, as Euphrasia appeared in flowing white robes with a scarlet sash, her arms modestly covered by flesh-coloured silk gloves and with a gold-trimmed helmet on her head. Fanny acted 'Portia' in *The Merchant of Venice* in 1830 wearing a costume that looked, according to her own description, 'like a gown made of strawberries and cream'.

Turning to the subject of everyday dress, it should be noted that the somewhat straight *skirt*, widening slightly towards the hem and made on similar lines to the diagram shown in Fig. 21, and the short *bodice*, were still in vogue in 1820, but other details of costume showed numerous modifications. Except in the case of ball dresses (which were cut low both front and back), the bodice was worn high at the

neck, with short sleeves gathered in puffs at the top. These short
puffed sleeves were sometimes inset in a long gauze sleeve reaching down
to the wrist. At other times the sleeves were charmingly ornamented
with interlaced trimming of the same materials as the dress (see
Plate VI). The skirt was fairly short, and often hardly reached the

Fig. 45. 'Juliet' 1829

ankle. Although white was still much worn, the reign of George IV
witnessed an increasing tendency in favour of strong-coloured dresses.
Coloured bodices were also frequently worn with white skirts.

In 1824, the prohibition on foreign silks was withdrawn and ulti-
mately abolished. In point of fact the prevalence of smuggling had
already made the prohibition practically valueless. Balzarine, a cotton

and wool mixture, and cotton delaine, a thickish soft muslin, were popular materials in 1830.

From 1821 onwards, dresses assumed a longer waist and skirts gained in fullness, being worn over a starched or thickly padded *petticoat* (see Fig. 46). Sometimes the petticoat was made of stiff drill with

Fig. 46. Ball Dress 1825

several flounces. At the same time a slightly longer bodice appeared, and short STAYS returned to favour after being altogether banished for more than twenty years.

A smart *walking dress* is shown in Plate VIII, carried out in cherry-coloured *gros de Naples*. The bodice, open in front over a straw-coloured chemisette, is decorated with piped points and folds of the same material, giving a fichu effect. The jockies on the shoulders are also edged with piped points. The full sleeves of straw-coloured lawn finish at the wrists with cuffs *en suite*. The deep false hem of the skirt is headed with piped angular *motifs* and a narrow panel descends the front. The scarf is of French grey sarcenet worked with silk and fringe in a deeper tone. The ensemble is completed by a hat similar to that described on page 59, of the same cherry colour as the dress, and is adorned with three paradise plumes and wide ribbons but no shoulder ends.

At the beginning of this period a fichu-shaped chemisette was some-times worn with a low-necked bodice, and was termed a 'CANEZOU'. It was frequently decorated with tucks or narrow ruchings. Pointed belt *corselets* in some cases took the place of sash or waistband.

SLEEVES. In 1823 the gathered shoulder first appeared, and about 1827 the sleeves were set lower, thus giving a sloping appearance to the bodice. From 1825 onwards, scalloped frills and trimmings were much in vogue. Sleeves were also worn fuller, and the year 1827 saw the first appearance of the '*ham-shaped sleeve*', enormously wide at the top and narrowing from the elbow to the wrist (see Fig. 47).

TRIMMINGS. From 1827 onwards, skirts frequently had decorated borders of varied design, both simple and elaborate.

COURT DRESS. On ascending the throne in 1820, George IV abolished that monstrosity, the hoop, from the Court dress. During his reign this ceremonial costume was modelled on lines similar to those adopted in France under Louis XVIII (see Fig. 32). In England, as in France, the Court train was now a separate item distinct from the dress. Drawing-rooms were held in the morning during this and the following reigns.

Fig. 48 is an English Court dress of 1821, in the mode established after the abolition of the hoop. The dress is carried out in white satin, the bodice and sleeves almost entirely composed of point lace, and is girded high with a silver ceinture. The skirt is cut on fashionable lines and finished at the hem with elaborately piped and puffed rouleaux in pale pink satin. The pink satin train depending from the ceinture is similarly embellished. The headdress consists of a jewelled coronet, lace lappets in the French fashion, and a panache of white ostrich-plumes. Elbow-length gloves are worn.

Spencers and pelisses continued to be worn, often with a long sleeve coming down from within a short puffed or ruched upper sleeve (see Fig. 49). The upper sleeve gradually disappeared with the development of full-top sleeves in 1824.

The *redingote* was still worn both for outdoor and evening wear.

Fig. 50 depicts a smart evening gown of embroidered muslin over white satin, with transparent muslin sleeves reaching to the wrist, with which was worn a green velvet redingote bordered with white fur in the Polish fashion, and a velvet toque or turban edged with fur and surmounted by a paradise plume.

Fig. 47. Day Dress 1827

GLOVES and MITTENS were still in general use. Green gloves were considered very chic. With the advent of the long sleeve, a shorter glove was naturally worn, but a fairly long glove still remained popular for evening wear.

NECKWEAR. From 1820 onwards, women were again wearing a fairly broad neck-ruff, called the '*fraise*', with high-necked dresses (see Fig. 49). With low-necked evening gowns necklets of pearls or small gold chains were used (see Fig. 46). About 1827 the ruff gave place to a flat shoulder-cape with a narrow frill at the top. This was

Fig. 48. Court Dress 1821

worn with both high- and low-necked dresses. The gathered *berthe* of lace or silk was another variation, although it had not yet reached the peak of popularity. Light *gauze scarves* were worn in summer, and in winter were replaced by *fur boas* consisting of numerous pieces

of fur threaded together on a long cord. Fur boas were also worn in
the evening.

FOOTWEAR. The shoe with rounded toe remained general until 1830,
when it was superseded by a square-toed shape. Shoes were still

Fig. 49. Redingote 1822   Fig. 50. Polish Redingote 1820

worn without heels, and secured by narrow ribbons crossed and tied
round the ankle. A tiny rosette or bow often decorated the instep.
Boots without heels were also in use. These, laced at the side, had
a seam down the front, and a leather toe-cap.

HEADDRESSES. The bonnet, in various forms, was the general head-

covering throughout the twenties.   The most popular was a silk bonnet
with the brim curving in at the front, the sides being drawn together
by ribbons tied in a bow under the chin.   A high-crowned *poke-bonnet*
of straw material was also worn.

Large, broad-brimmed hats, tied beneath the chin with broad fancy
ribbon and decorated with ribbons and feathers or flowers, were worn
in Paris before the year 1824.   When these large hats first made their
appearance, the brims were turned down all round.   In 1827 the hat

Fig. 51. Fashionable Coiffure

was worn tilted on one side, and became a very flat, wide-brimmed
piece of head-gear decorated with a profusion of ribbons, loops of
ribbons, ostrich feathers, and paradise plumes.   The chin ribbons
were usually worn untied, one hanging in front and the other behind
the shoulder.   Plate VIII shows a fashionable young woman wearing
one of these modish hats.

Caps with pointed frills and puffs were worn indoors, and feathered
plumes were still in fashion for the evening.

HAIRDRESSING. The hair was still worn parted in the centre with
a cluster of curls drawn to each side of the face.   The back hair was
arranged in plaits or curls on top of the head.   Towards 1830 these
back curls were gathered into stiff loops kept in position with a high
comb (see Figs. 51 and 52).

BAGS AND SACHETS were made in tulle, chenille, and coloured silks. They were sometimes painted or embroidered in ribbon-work.

FANS were of two varieties, some very small of painted silk, and others of a larger kind made of feathers.

MUFFS were still of large size and often ornamented in front by a bow with long ends.

PARASOLS were in use of the same varieties as in the preceding period.

Fig. 52. Coiffure 1829

Some were more convex than others, and frequently fringe not only appeared at the edge but also surrounded the stick where it protruded through the top of the parasol. Parasols, when closed, were carried by the end as frequently as by the handle. *Umbrellas* were of normal size.

LIST OF ARTISTS WORKING DURING THIS AND THE FOLLOWING REIGN

William Beechey	1753–1839
Thomas Lawrence	1769–1830
Francis Chantrey	1781–1841
David Wilkie	1785–1841
George Hayter	1792–1871
George Cruikshank	1792–1878
Paul Gavarni	1801–1866

CHAPTER III

REIGN OF WILLIAM IV (1830–37)

CONTEMPORARY FOREIGN GOVERNMENTS

FRANCE: Louis-Philippe, King of the French (1830–48)
PRUSSIA: Frederick William III (1797–1840)
AUSTRIA: Francis I (1804–35)
Ferdinand I (1835–48)
RUSSIA: Nicholas I (1825–55)
SPAIN: Ferdinand VII (1814–33)
Isabella II (1833–70)
Regency of Queen Maria Christina (1833–43)
ITALY: Various Independent Governments

INTRODUCTION

WILLIAM HENRY, DUKE OF CLARENCE, was the third son of King George III, and was born 21st August 1765. He married, 11th July 1818, Adelaide, Princess of Saxe-Meiningen, who died in 1849.

The coronation of King William IV, the Sailor King, September 1831, was extremely simple compared with that of George IV. In full state King William wore the uniform of an admiral and over it the Mantle of the Order of the Garter or Parliamentary robes. In ordinary day life he dressed as a private citizen. Mr. Saunders of Brighton said in 1903: 'I remember William IV quite well. I saw him enter Brighton for the first time. I remember he had rather coarse features with a heavy jowl. He used to wear Hessian boots, drab breeches, blue coat, and yellow waistcoat'.

A portrait in possession of His Majesty King George V shows King William wearing a dark cloth, double-breasted, brass-buttoned, square tail-coat, with normal-sized sleeves extending well over the hand. The coat has cloth lapels and a high, rolled velvet collar. Black stock with narrow white collar turned down over the top. The trousers are a little lighter in tone than the coat, and are a trifle baggy. The Star of the Order of Guelphs is suspended from a blue ribbon at the neck and the Star of the Garter is on the coat. Lemon-yellow kid gloves are worn, and a top-hat carried under the left arm. The black boots are highly varnished (see Fig. 53).

When walking, William IV usually carried an umbrella under his arm, a commonplace habit, no doubt, which is scarcely in accordance

Fig. 53. King William IV

with the generally accepted idea of kingship. Neither does the following description of him by Washington Irving suggest great dignity! 'His Majesty has an easy and natural way of wiping his nose with the back of his forefinger which, I fancy, is a relic of his old middy habit.'

Life in the Royal circle during this reign was more subdued in comparison with that of the Regency and the preceding reign. The tenderness and sweetness of Queen Adelaide helped to soften the somewhat crude manners of the time, and the Court began to breathe a more refined and respectable atmosphere. The King had sown all his wild oats, and reaped their harvest, before he was unexpectedly called to the throne. By this time he was satisfied to lead a quiet domestic life. Nevertheless his language was considerably unrestrained, possibly as the result of his long service in the navy.

William IV died at Windsor, 20th June 1837. His last words were: 'Doctor, I know I am going, but I should like to see another anniversary of Waterloo. Try if you cannot tinker me up to last over that day!'

MEN'S COSTUME

London was still the centre of masculine fashion, and indeed remained so for the rest of the century. Count D'Orsay, although a Frenchman, may be considered the leader of English fashion at this time. He certainly took Beau Brummell's place in London Society. Alfred Guillaume Gabriel D'Orsay was the son of General Comte D'Orsay, and was born in Paris in 1801. He was a tall, handsome man, with an exceptionally fine figure which enabled him to wear his clothes to the best possible advantage. His sister was the beautiful Duchesse de Guiche. Henri IV and Louis XV were patrons only of bridges across the Seine, but an ancestor of the count's gave his name to a whole quay on the bank of that river. Count D'Orsay was famous for his faultless style, the perfection of his wardrobe, and his efforts at portrait-painting. Fig. 54 is made from a drawing of the count, and shows him in everyday walking attire. The neckcloth is entirely of black satin, made to fit the neck and breast in a series of nonchalant folds. The single-breasted waistcoat has a roll collar and is slightly pointed at the waist. It should be noted that the double-breasted FROCK COAT is worn open and thrown well back over the shoulders. Gauntlet gloves are worn.

In this reign Benjamin Disraeli first came to the notice of the public. Born on 21st December 1804, he was the son of Isaac D'Israeli, 'an antiquary and bookworm, who, honourably preferring scholarship and poetry to money-making, abandoned the counting-house in which he had been started'.[1] While living with his father at Braden- ham House he heard, in 1832, that there was a political vacancy in the

---

[1] Margaret M. Verney.

neighbouring borough of High Wycombe. 'Dizzy, the Younger', drove into the town in an open carriage-and-four. 'His hair was in long black curls, and he was dressed with his usual exuberance of lace shirt, flowered waistcoat, and coat with a pink lining.'

Fig. 54. Count D'Orsay 1834

Fig. 55 is a drawing of Disraeli at this period. The pleated cuffs which he wears were unusual at this time, being a personal idiosyncrasy of the aspiring politician. The long black curls were also an exaggeration of contemporary fashion affected by smart young men about town.

COATS in general were similar to those worn in the preceding reign, the only modifications being the lengthening of the waist and widening of tails. The waist was still tight, and all well-dressed men wore *corsets*. Velvet collars and cuffs were still the vogue.

Both the *swallow-tail coat* (see Fig. 56) and a *coat with a square*

Fig. 55. Benjamin Disraeli 1833

skirt were considered correct (see Figs. 55 and 57). The tail-coat held its own for evening wear. Ordinary day coats were of dark colours but the tone of the smartest coats was decidedly brighter in colour.

WAISTCOATS, single breasted, with or without lapels, were more generally worn. For evening wear the waistcoat was cut lower. In 1836 the roll collar appeared on the waistcoat, and the upper edge of the waistcoat was folded outward in uniform width as far as the breast. In colour they were strong and were made of many kinds of fancy materials—velvet and cashmere being considered very smart. Often two waistcoats were worn, a dark one under a light or white one. It was now

Fig. 56. Prince Orsini 1834   Fig. 57. William Harrison Ainsworth 1832

the custom to carry the watch in the left hand pocket of the waiscoat, and suspended from the neck by a small gold chain.

From 1836 *sleeves* were made as tight as possible, and generally reached only to the wrist, the shoulders being less padded and more pointed.

A very smart *double-breasted coat* is shown in Fig. 58. The full

skirts are cut away in front, the front edges, cut rather on the slope,
fall back revealing the silk lining.   This particular coat and lapels are
of bottle-green cloth, the skirts lined with black satin, and the high

Fig. 58. Gentleman 1836

collar of black velvet.   A purple satin stock over a white waistcoat,
stone-coloured trousers, and a black, smooth beaver hat are worn.

In April 1832, it was decreed that: 'For gentlemen's dress coats and
frocks the bright mulberry and French brown of a red shade are now
fashionable.   Velvet collars and facings are much used for both coats.

Of course, neither of these colours is intended for full dress, which must be either black or blue '.

Very full-skirted *greatcoats* were worn (see Figs. 59 and 60), as well as long *Italian capes* with high turn-over collars. *Cloaks* for use when riding had a slit at the back that could be buttoned at will. By 1830

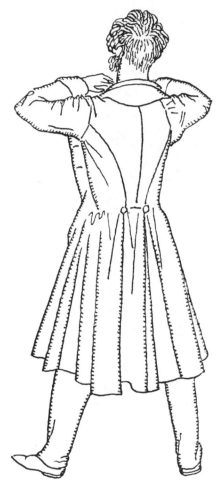

Fig. 59. Edward Bulwer, Lord Lytton, 1832

the various overcapes on the cloak had grown longer, but less numerous. Towards 1837 the fashionable cloak was considerably shorter and lighter.

NECKWEAR. Plain black stocks or cravats, with or without a bow in front, were worn as in the preceding reign. For these, satin was the most favoured, although cravats were sometimes made of camlet or serge, and a backing of stiffening material was universally employed.

The upstanding points of the collar were sometimes, but not always, visible. A frilled or soft pleated shirtfront completed the ensemble.

BREECHES AND TROUSERS. Very tight ankle-length breeches or trousers buttoned up the calf were still worn, as well as plain trousers fastened

Fig. 60. Gentleman 1837

by a strap beneath the boot (see Figs. 55 and 57). *Knee-breeches* and ankle-length *pantaloons* of silk or stockinette were both popular for evening wear. After 1835, trousers showed a tendency to widen. The chief materials employed were twill and corduroy, and in summer coarse cotton or East Indian nankeen. White buckskin was the usual wear for riding. *Court dress* of this reign is described in Chapter V, page 142.

CLOTHES FOR YOUNG BOYS. A modification of the '*Dutch skeleton dress*' was still in use. See page 49. Sometimes, however, instead of a coat or jacket, a blouse was worn and tucked inside the high-waisted trousers. The sleeves were frequently ornamented with frills and ruchings (see Plate IX). The frilled collar still persisted.

FOOTWEAR. Boots and shoes were squared-toed and rather long and

Fig. 61. Bonnet   Fig. 62. Hat

narrow. Short boots of the Wellington type were still popular, and were worn beneath the trousers.

A newspaper of the period states that 'The name of Wellington is no longer seen attached to articles for sale. Everything that bore the name has been changed, Wellington boots are now called *Reform boots*'. Top-boots were worn with riding kit. *Shoes* for indoor wear were ornamented with a bow or buckle (see Fig. 55).

HEADGEAR. The top-hat was almost universal, and was generally high and straight. Some hats, however, were distinguished by a tapered crown and larger brim. Caps were still sometimes worn for convenience, and were of various types, such as the *Orleans cap*, the *Russian cap*, and the *Austrian cap*. Nearly all these varieties more or less resembled the Tam-o'-shanter.   A cap with a black peak projecting from a tartan band was much worn by young boys (see Plate IX).

HAIRDRESSING. The hair was worn rather long, generally parted on the left side, but occasionally in the centre.   Curls on top or at the sides were highly prized and the hair was often crimped to obtain the desired effect (see Fig. 56).   The face was usually clean-shaven with the exception of short *side-whiskers*.

SMOKING. The habit of smoking became much more general during this

Fig. 63. Shoulder Capes

reign owing to the duty on the importation of cigars being much reduced.

Great quantities of phosphorus matches, imported from Germany, were now on sale all over the Continent.

WOMEN'S COSTUME

At the beginning of the thirties, a *bodice* with a pointed front was sometimes worn (see Fig. 51, and Plate X).   The neck was cut very low, but except for evening wear the shoulders were covered by *capes* or *fichus* of tulle or fine embroidery.   These capes were often worn two or three deep and were elaborately frilled (see Fig. 61).   The V-shaped *berthe* enjoyed great popularity throughout the whole of this period.

Contemporaneously with the pointed variety was a bodice whose chief feature was a *waistband* ornamented with a round or square buckle (see Figs. 62 and 63). *Shoulder capes* were now lengthened in front and behind, the long points being kept in place by the waistband.

All dresses at this time fastened at the back, but with them were

Fig. 64. Riding Habit 1835

sometimes worn *overdresses* fastening in front and reaching well up to the neck.

RIDING HABITS. From time immemorial it was a necessity for women to ride as a means of travel and sport. In the early years of the nineteenth century it was the fashion to ride for the sake of effect, consequently the riding habit received much thought and attention. Thoroughfares for the parade of horsemanship were made in the chief cities of the

Continent.   Fig. 64 shows the type of riding habit fashionable during this reign.   It is of coloured cloth, with sloping shoulders, turned down cambric and lace collar *à la Vandyke* and bouffant sleeves.   The skirt

Fig. 65. Carriage Dress, July 1832

is cut extra full to set well when the wearer is mounted.   A masculine top hat, of black or coloured beaver, is draped with a blue gauze veil which is expected to float gracefully in the breeze.   The gloves of white kid have the edge of the gauntlet cut in points and embroidered with gold.

CARRIAGE DRESSES. Driving for pleasure and show had been indulged in for nearly a hundred years. This habit became much more general at the dawn of the nineteenth century. The great improvements made in the coachmaker's craft, and the comfort and lightness of the most up-to-date carriages, encouraged Society to take their airings in good style upon the newly constructed carriage ways, which began to appear in all the important cities of Europe. Frequent mention, and many drawings of carriage dresses, are to be found in fashion books of this time.

Fig. 65 is a *carriage dress* of 1832 in pink-striped *gros de Naples* and jaconet muslin. The *corsage* of the pelisse fits close to the shape and is very open in front, displaying a simple *chemisette* of cambric. The lapels which fall back are divided on the shoulders, square across the back, and are edged with a *torsage* of pink and white silk and a white *rouleau*. The jockey (or wide epaulette) is of the same material as the dress, and falls over the upper part of the full white sleeve in deep points edged with white. The skirt is left very open to show the embroidered flounce of the underskirt. It is trimmed down the front with a *torsage*, a white *rouleau*, and a row of points increasing in depth gradually downwards. The hat is of straw-coloured *moiré* trimmed with gauze ribbon delicately striped with brown. A bow is placed near the hair on each side, an end of each is brought across the brim and united on the upper part within an inch of the edge, where they form another bow a little on one side. The ornament on the crown is of cut ends and bows, in imitation of a flower with its leaves.

In connection with the subject of transport, it should be noted that the steam-engine was perfected and railways were being laid during this reign. There were first-class carriages on the trains, but it was not unusual for an elegant crane-neck landau, mounted on a railway truck and occupied by some very smart ladies and gentlemen, with footmen seated with folded arms in the rumble, to be attached to the London and Greenwich train.

COURT DRESS. A Court dress of 1832 is shown in Fig. 66, and is constructed on the fashionable lines of that year. The following description of it is taken from a contemporary magazine:

A robe of white satin trimmed with blonde, flounces set diagonally; each finished with a bunch of moss roses. The body is profusely ornamented with blonde and pearls. On each shoulder is placed a rose similar to those which decorate the skirt.   Train of ponceau satin, richly embroidered with embossed silver; it is fastened on round the waist with a band of pearls, from which depends a cordelière finished with two tassels of pearls. Headdress; diamonds and emeralds, with a plume of ostrich feathers, and mantilla of blonde.   White satin gloves; shoes of silver tissue.

It should be mentioned that 'ponceau' was the name for the fashion-

Fig. 66. Court Dress 1832

able colour—poppy red. Also that the flounces of blonde lace which fall over the very large ponceau satin sleeves continue across the back, forming a kind of cape.

CORONATION ROBES. Fig. 67 shows the costume worn by

Fig. 67. Queen Adelaide 1831

Queen Adelaide at her coronation, 8th September 1831. It was evidently the model from which the preceding was copied. The dress is of white satin, embroidered in a diaper design of groups of three oak-leaves. Gold embroideries decorate the body, and flounces of lace are draped over the sleeves and décolletage. The long train of purple velvet, bordered with heavy gold lace, is attached round the waist by a gold and jewelled ornament.   The beautiful lace veil is surmounted by the crown matrimonial of Great Britain, and the sceptre is carried in the white-gloved hand.

A charming full-length portrait of this queen was painted by Sir William Beechey (1753–1839) early in the reign, and is possessed by the Elder Brethren of Trinity House.   A three-quarter-length replica by the same artist is in the National Portrait Gallery, London.   It shows this amiable lady in a plain dress of deep blue velvet made on simple fashionable lines with large white blonde-lace sleeves.   The coiffure is very much of the period, and from the back hangs a veil of the same filmy lace.

Miss Clitherow states that Queen Adelaide encouraged home manufacture by wearing all things English.   'Her dress was so moderate, sleeves and headdress much less than the hideous fashion.'

SLEEVES. At the beginning of William IV's reign, the chief characteristic was the long '*ham-shaped sleeve*', enormously wide at the top, and narrowing from the elbow down to the wrist.   These sleeves, as well as the short *puffed sleeves* of ball dresses (see Plate X), were kept at full width by wicker frames or feather cushions.   BALL DRESSES were often embellished by '*volants*', or ruffles, of lace or embroidery hanging from the short puffed sleeves (see Fig. 51, and Plate X).   Towards 1835, a big round sleeve came into vogue, sometimes tightly pleated into quarters.   Another variation of the middle thirties was a reversal of the ham-shaped sleeve, now worn tight at the top and wide lower down.   It was still gathered in at the wrist, but the fullness of the sleeve often fell over the wristband.   In 1837 there was a distinct tendency to tighter sleeves, neatly gathered well down the shoulders.   Sleeves and bodices alike were often decorated with bows and ruchings (see Plate XI).

Very wide *epaulette collars* were a noticeable feature.   These met in a V-shape at the waist, revealing the top of a lace or embroidered *chemisette* worn beneath.   Sometimes these chemisettes were of pleated tulle or muslin with a narrow frill round the neck.   Bodices were usually lined with white or grey half-linen, and stiffened with whalebone. *Stays* were also worn.

NECKWEAR. There was a greater variety of neck ornament than of neckwear about 1830.   For evening wear plain, broad, gold chains were worn, or small gold chains connected with diamonds or other precious stones (see Fig. 51).   Sufficient mention has already been made of the numerous fancy capes with pointed frills which were worn with morning and afternoon dresses.

SKIRTS. At the beginning of the reign, skirts were rather short and very full, being worn over stiff flounced petticoats (see Plate X). The skirts themselves were sometimes decorated with one or two flounces

Fig. 68. Pelisse or Pelerine 1836

and loopings of flowers. Bows and ruches were other favourite trimmings. Braid was also considerably used for decorative purposes, and some of the dresses had a pleasing arrangement of tassels down the front. Towards 1837 skirts showed a tendency to lengthen, and the ankles were seldom visible (see Plate XI).

A kind of overdress called the 'POLONAISE' was often worn, and this garment was caught up here and there with posies of artificial flowers. *Pelisses* of rather strong colours maintained their popularity and were now frequently ornamented with braid.

Fig. 68 shows a 'PUBLIC PROMENADE DRESS' consisting of a *pelisse* or PELERINE of emerald-green satin trimmed with swansdown down the front and round the border. The corsage made high and tight to the shape (a contemporary expression meaning 'figure') is finished round the throat with a rouleau of swansdown. There are long, tight sleeves trimmed at the wrists *en suite*. Over this is worn a *mantelet à la capuchon*, of the same material as the pelisse, surrounded by swansdown and lined with pink satin. The bonnet (often referred to in fashion books as 'a hat') is of pink satin with blonde lace frill inside.

CLOAKS AND MANTLES. Heavy capes and mantles were much worn in winter, and, like the pelisse, were often trimmed with braid. The cloak of the period closely resembled an overcoat, the only differences being the greater width of the garment and the addition of a long cape. After a while the sleeves were omitted, and the garment again became a mere '*wrap*', by which name it was often known.

SHAWLS AND SCARVES were still continuously worn, but the fur boas of the preceding reign had generally gone out of fashion. About 1835 *mantillas* reappeared, almost completely ousting both the shawl and scarf. At first, these mantillas resembled those of the later eighteenth century, and were usually made of black silk and often trimmed with ruching. After a time they became shorter at the back and wider across the shoulders, more nearly resembling a short cape with loose ends.

UNDERCLOTHES. Mention has already been made of the lace or embroidered *chemisette*, and the stiff flounced *petticoat*. It was now customary to wear at least two or three petticoats, in contrast to the single diaphanous petticoat of the first decade of the century. *Stays* or *corsets* were a necessity in order to achieve the fashionable tight waist. Long-legged DRAWERS or *pantalettes*, trimmed with lace, were also universally worn. The somewhat abbreviated dress worn by young girls of the period allowed the pantalettes to peep forth from beneath the billowy skirts (see Plate IX).

FOOTWEAR. Shoes were of the low sandal type, without heels, and fastened across the instep by crossed elastic or ribbon (see Plate X). A square toe was fashionable, and the front part of the shoe was sometimes decorated with a small rosette or bow. Ankle-boots were also worn, usually laced inside, and having long patent-leather toe-caps. A fashion book of August 1837 informs its readers that '*Brodequins* (or *half-boots*) are much in vogue this season'. Apart from the toe-cap, leather was rarely used, both boots and shoes being made of cloth or silk.

HEADDRESSES showed a good deal of variety during this reign. *The coal-scuttle bonnet* was still popular (see Plate XI, and Figs. 61, 68, and 69), but the brim in front was now made as round as possible, and a high crown was worn to accommodate the exaggerated loops of hair. The favourite trimmings for bonnets were flowers, ribbons, and paradise plumes (see aforesaid illustrations). *The large, flat, circular hat*, worn

Fig. 69. Bonnet

rather on the back of the head, or tilted on one side, and lavishly decorated with feathers, flowers, and bows (see Plate VIII, and in Fig. 62), which came in about 1827, was now very fashionable. For riding, a hat was often worn resembling the masculine top-hat, with the addition of a long veil looped round the crown and hanging down the back. Another variety worn with riding dress was a flat *tam-o'-shanter* shape with a large peak in front, very like the masculine cap.

HAIRDRESSING. The back hair was still gathered on top into a series of stiff, high loops kept up with wire frames and held in position by an ornamental comb. The hair in front was parted in the middle or at the side, and spread out into clusters of curls on both sides of the head and face (see Plate X, and Fig. 66). On ceremonial occasions, artificial puffs were added. These were stiffened with wire and attached to the head as high as possible by means of small, long-toothed combs. The whole structure was further embellished with loops of ribbon or flowers and feathers (see Figs. 51 and 52).   Sometimes the hair in front, instead of being smoothly parted, was curled all over into elaborate puffs. This style of coiffure was usually worn with the large circular hat (see Fig. 62).   Children wore the hair parted in the centre, smoothly combed to the sides and plaited, the ends of the plaits being caught up on to the head with small bows (see Plate IX).

PARASOLS AND UMBRELLAS retained the same shapes and sizes, as described in the last chapter.

HANDBAGS of a curved form were mostly favoured and were generally decorated with heavy tassels.   FANS were very small, and a round shape was sometimes used.   Gilt BOUQUET-HOLDERS with pearl handles were much in vogue.   GLOVES and MITTENS continued as in the preceding reign.   LORGNETTES were now adopted by women of fashion.

CHAPTER IV

EARLY VICTORIAN PERIOD (1837–57)

CONTEMPORARY FOREIGN GOVERNMENTS

FRANCE: Louis-Philippe, King of the French (1830–48)
          The Second Republic (1848–52)
          The Second Empire, Napoleon III (1852–70)

PRUSSIA: Frederick William III (1797–1840)
          Frederick William IV (1840–61)

AUSTRIA: Ferdinand I (1835–48)
          Francis-Joseph (1848–1916)

RUSSIA: Nicholas I (1825–55)
          Alexander II (1855–81)

SPAIN: Isabella II (1833–70)
          Regency of Queen Maria Christina (1833–43)

ITALY: Various Independent Governments

INTRODUCTION

ALEXANDRINA VICTORIA only child of Edward, Duke of Kent, and Victoria Maria-Louisa of Saxe-Coburg-Saalfeld, was born at Kensington Palace 24th May 1819. She ascended the throne as Queen Victoria 20th June 1837, and was crowned at Westminster the following year.

Greville speaks of the young Queen as having 'perfect calmness and self-possession' and 'graceful modesty and propriety'. Her mother, the Duchess of Kent, was not on friendly terms with the late king, consequently, their visits to Windsor were not frequent. Brought up very quietly, and with much circumspection, she became popular with her uncle, King William, who had a great regard for his niece, but to the public in general the young princess was scarcely known. When she ascended the throne at the age of eighteen, there was a great deal of curiosity among her subjects as to the personality of the young woman who was to reign over them.

Queen Victoria married, at St. James's Palace in 1840, Albert, second son of Ernest, Duke of Saxe-Coburg and Gotha, born at Rosenau 26th August 1819. With regard to the Court, the young queen continued the good work commenced by her aunt, Queen Adelaide, consequently the tone of Society in general much improved after the beginning of the reign.   Both men and women were much more discreet in their behaviour and in their speech.   An authority [1] on these matters states that

Old statesmen who had enjoyed life in a very unrestrained fashion sought to impose a higher standard of social morality upon Society once the Queen had begun to reign.   Lord Melbourne, whose conversation had previously been interlarded with a multitude of 'Damns', became the pink of colloquial propriety, in addition to which he took care that only those who (outwardly at least) were noted for their unimpeachable morality should have access to the queen's presence.

This influence spread from the Court throughout all ranks of Society; and this high morality continued and greatly increased as time went on.

Commencing with a great and far-reaching measure of Reform, the middle classes, at the beginning of this reign, initiated their struggle for political ascendency with some success, but on the whole, the governing classes maintained their supremacy.

During the entire Victorian era, London Society witnessed the regime of a succession of eminent hostesses.   The Countess of Blessington held supreme sway in 'High Life' during the early years of the reign and among the habitués of her salon were Prince Louis Napoleon (afterwards Napoleon III of France); the Dukes of Beaufort, Bedford, Hamilton, Montrose, and Somerset; the Marquis of Londonderry; the Earls of Chesterfield, Durham, Eglinton, Erroll, and Scarborough; Count d'Orsay, Bulwer Lytton, Disraeli, Walter Savage Landor, Albany Fonblanque, and Alfred de Vigny.

Among the many notabilities who influenced Society in the forties was the Countess of Jersey, wife of the fifth earl, and daughter of the Earl of Westmorland.   She was a *grande dame* in every sense of the word.   Her daughter, Lady Clementina, was one of the queen's bridesmaids.

Society's interest in fancy dress continued to be a feature of the period stimulated by the Romantic Movement in literature associated with the names of Victor Hugo, Scott, and the elder Dumas.   In this connection may be mentioned the Eglinton Tournament held in 1839 which was based on the description of the tourney at Ashby de la Zouch in 'Ivanhoe' (pub. 1821).   Sir Walter Scott took as his authority Jean Froissart (1337–1410) but introduced some considerably inaccurate details of his own.   Like most out-of-door entertainments it was a failure owing to the uncertain English weather.   From an artistic point of view it was a success, if we disregard the fact that the

[1] Ralph Nevill.

ladies wore their sideless gowns over innumerable voluminuos petti-coats: a predominating feature of their headdresses was the smoothly plastered hair over the temples. The chin whiskers of the gentlemen were much in evidence. It was a noble thought of the Earl of Eglinton to revive this interesting historic contest, but, as was said at the time, it was doomed to failure as the very ethics of the institution were so totally at variance with the sentiment prevailing in those times.

From mock combats we turn to real ones. It is interesting to note that in 1844 the last duel on record took place between Colonel D. L. Fawcett and Lieutenant Munro. The latter was killed, and the former fled the country.

The Great Exhibition of the Industry of All Nations, held in Hyde Park in 1851 at the instigation of Prince Albert, was talked of then, and for many years afterwards, as the greatest wonder that had ever been seen. The architect of the Crystal Palace built to house the exhibits was Sir Joseph Paxton (1803–65), who was also a landscape gardener. He laid out the grounds surrounding the Exhibition. The contractors were Messrs. Fox and Henderson. The decoration of the interior was entrusted to that skilled authority on the subject, Owen Jones (1809–1874). Such was the extraordinary eagerness to be present at the exhibition inauguration on the 1st May that forty thousand pounds' worth of season tickets were sold before the 29th April. The influence of the Exhibition was far-reaching and affected textiles, furniture, and all objects of art, for British manufacturers were then made to realize the low standard in taste and artistic design of their goods in comparison with the productions of foreign competitors. The Great Exhibition created a 'New Art', but of a somewhat debased kind. This is realized if one examines the illustrations in the official catalogue published at the time. The exhibits must have presented a heterogeneous collection of appalling monstrosities!

Furniture and interior decoration chiefly suffered and this debasement took place approximately between the years 1830–75. During this period, furniture of the seventeenth and eighteenth centuries was considered 'old-fashioned' and out-of-date and destroyed or relegated to the servants' quarters or the stable. Vandalism in churches was another crime committed during the middle of the nineteenth century chiefly by the clergy in their well-meaning but ignorant desire for 'restoration'.

A prominent juror of the Exhibition of 1851 was Augustus Welby Northmore Pugin, son of Augustin Pugin (1762–1832), a Frenchman who came to London after the Revolution and worked in the office of John

Nash the architect.   The younger Pugin, born in 1812, became a distinguished architect, an ardent Roman Catholic, and the originator of that particular style of architecture known as 'Victorian Gothic'.   Dying in 1852 he was succeeded by his son, Edward Welby Pugin (1834–75).

The architect most useful to students of furniture, costume, and armour, was a Frenchman, Eugène Emmanuel Viollet-le-Duc.   Born in 1814, his writings on these subjects are considered *chefs-d'œuvre* of erudition and æsthetics.   He died in 1879.

Wax candles in cut-glass, silver, and sometimes gold, candlesticks or candelabra were the only means of artificial lighting in use up to the first years of Queen Victoria's reign.   Mutton-fat candles, dip candles and rushlights were humbler alternatives.   An innovation in interior lighting was the introduction of oil lamps about the commencement of this reign.   As time progressed great improvements were made in oil lamps and many ingenious devices were introduced, some emanating from the practical mind of Prince Albert.   H.R.H. also brought back from Germany the newest kind of oil lamp, fitted with a green shade, to protect his eyes when reading: this he always used.

An interesting source of study for costume is the daguerreotype, a picture or portrait produced by a process invented by a French painter named Daguerre in 1839.   This style of portrait remained in vogue until the art of photography was introduced in 1841.   After an Exhibition of Photography held in 1852 persons in High Life had their likenesses taken and mounted on cards two and a half by four inches called 'Cartes de Visite'.   Figs. 128 and 163 are drawn from such photographs.

MEN'S COSTUME

In this period one does not hear so much of the supreme dandy as in the preceding reigns.   There were, of course, men of fashion and fashionably dressed men, but there was no pre-eminent arbiter of masculine fashion.   Count D'Orsay, it is true, held his own during the early part of the reign, but after his death in 1852 there was no indisputable successor to wear his cloak.   One of the few dressy young men of this time was Disraeli.

'"Young Dizzy" made his maiden speech in the House of Commons, 1837, garbed in a bottle green frock coat, and waistcoat covered with a network of glittering chains, large fancy patterned pantaloons and a black stock without shirt collar.'   He looked 'tall and thin, with a countenance lividly pale, intensely black eyes, his broad forehead overhung by long flowing ringlets of coal black hair'. His style at this time was somewhat similar to that of Count d'Orsay as shown in Fig. 54 (Chapter III). At a later date Disraeli is described as wearing a black

Fig. 70. H.R.H. Prince Albert 1840

velvet coat lined with white satin. Evidently the former material was a favourite with the eminent statesman, for photographs of him in a black velvet coat bound with black braid, but without the white satin lining, are often seen.

For an EVENING DRESS suit of the period, a smart example is

shown in Fig. 70, taken from a portrait of Prince Albert painted in 1840. The sprigged waistcoat is somewhat unusual in conjunction with evening dress, although it was commonly in use for everyday wear.   His Royal Highness wears the Star of the Hanoverian Order of Guelph hung on

Fig. 71. Prince Louis Napoleon 1848

a sky-blue ribbon at the neck, the Star of the Garter on the left breast, and the ribbon with lesser George across the shoulder.   For orthodox *Court dress* of this period refer to Fig. 119 (Chapter V).

Fig. 71 is a drawing of Louis Napoleon (afterwards Napoleon III), as 'Representative of the People' in 1848.   Prince Louis Napoleon, born in Paris, in 1808, was the son of Louis Bonaparte, King of

Holland, and Hortense de Beauharnais. He paid frequent visits to England between the years 1831 and 1848. He was elected Emperor of the French in November 1851. Not of great stature, he was none the less a fairly good dresser according to the idea of his time. He is

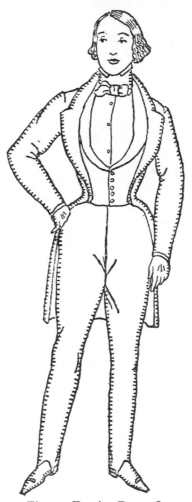

Fig. 72. Evening Dress 1845

shown in the illustration wearing ordinary everyday dress of a gentleman. There are also many illustrations of Prince Albert similarly garbed.

Up to 1841, the *dress-coat* was still worn unbuttoned, the tails being the same breadth at top and bottom, sharply cut away in front and squared at the foot. The collar was low and narrow, and the lapels extended nearly to the waist. The sleeves were tight and finished at the wrist, showing a small amount of white cuff. The gentleman in *evening dress* in Fig. 72 wears an ultra-fashionable dress coat of the period.

The frock coat was worn in 1840 with a tight waist and rather tight sleeves. It had back-pockets, deep lapels, and sometimes a velvet

Fig. 73. Day Dress 1850

collar (see Plate XII). About 1850 the upper part of both the dress coat and the ordinary coat increased in length, so that the high-waisted effect so long popular was now lost. At the same time the back became broader, the collar came higher up the neck in the front, and the sleeves were uniformly wide the full length of the arm (see Plate XIII). In the fifties, the MORNING COAT with rounded-off points at the skirt appeared. This coat also had a small collar and lapel. Square-cut JACKETS were also much in use by 1855, as well as complete *suits* in tweed or plaid (see Fig. 73).

Fig. 74. Sporting Kit 1855

The complete SPORTING KIT of the period is shown in Fig. 74. The grey double-breasted coat descends to the knees, and has two breast-pockets and a hip-pocket on each side. The rather flat collar is cut to show the full, knotted tie of crimson silk. Grey breeches are worn, and brown leather gaiters covering the instep strapped and buckled

up the outside of the leg.   The outfit is completed by a grey check
cap with a peak of the same, and black boots.

OVERCOATS of various types were worn in 1841, both single- and
double-breasted (see Figs. 75, 76, and 77).   The overcoat was some-

Fig. 75. Overcoat 1841   Fig. 76. Overcoat 1841

times cut to hang straight down from the shoulders, ending in a bell-
shape just above the knees (see Fig. 77), and sometimes fitted tightly
to the waist, the bell-shaped skirts being cut separately and reaching
half-way down the leg (see Fig. 76).   Most of these overcoats had
large flap pockets, and in some cases sported a small cape in addition

to the ordinary collar. The overcoat either buttoned right up to the neck, or was cut to reveal a portion of the cravat. Overcoats in 1855 were of several varieties, both loose- and tight-fitting (see Figs. 79

Fig. 77. Overcoat 1841   Fig. 78. Overcoat 1855

and 78). A loose, wide-sleeved coat, very popular at this time, was the 'RAGLAN', named after the commander of the English forces in the Crimea (see Fig. 79).

CLOAKS were still worn at the beginning of Victoria's reign, with or without an overcape, sometimes trimmed with fur (see Fig. 80). In the early forties the cloak gradually assumed the character of a coat. It was much shorter and closer fitting than formerly, and had two long openings at the level of the elbow through which the arms could

Fig. 79. The Raglan 1855

be passed. By 1850 it had entirely given place to the top-coat or overcoat.

WAISTCOATS. From 1837 onwards, waistcoats with a roll collar, either single- or double-breasted, were worn. Both plain and fancy materials were in use, and a sprigged or flowered design was frequently seen (Figs. 70 and 80). After a time, the waistcoat was made to button higher in the neck and also lost its high-waisted character. In 1850, fancy waistcoats were still worn (see Plate XIII). The lower edge was sometimes cut straight across in front, but more often finished in

Fig. 80. Cloak 1841

short points. After 1850, waistcoats were generally made of the same material as the coat or trousers (see Fig. 73). Velvet waistcoats were still occasionally worn, and in summer light waistcoats of washing material were much favoured. In the forties, a plain white single-breasted waistcoat with a roll collar was *de rigueur* in conjunction with a white tie for evening dress. This type of waistcoat is shown in Fig. 72.

NECKWEAR. In 1837 the *stock*, or *cravat*, usually of black satin with a bow in front, was still worn with a white frilled shirt-front showing above the waistcoat. The '*choker collar*' remained popular, but the pointed ends were no longer worn upright, and instead curved out on either side of the chin. Fig. 81 shows the two parts of half a collar. A B is seamed to D E. B C is the point in front, E F is the centre fold of

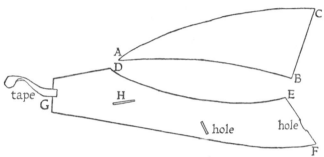

Fig. 81. Diagram of Collar

neckband. G is the end at the back with tapes which cross and pass through the holes on opposite sides, being tied through the hole in front of the band. The hole H is on the right side only. Cravats of white satin were usually worn at dances and other ceremonial occasions. By 1840 neckwear was almost entirely a matter of individual taste. Some men wore the cravat or stock, others wore a neckcloth, with or without a bow in front. *Neckcloths* for everyday wear were simply two broad pieces of dark material filling the open space at the top of the waistcoat, without a bow in front, being held together by buttons or pins (see Plate XII). By 1848 the elaborately tied stock or cravat had gradually gone out of fashion, its place being taken by a narrower *necktie* fastened in front by a pin or tied in a small bow or knot (see Plate XIII). A plain white shirt-front, devoid of frilling, was now visible above the waistcoat, and the tie itself was worn lower than the stock, so that part of the neck was seen between the pointed edges of the collar. About 1855 the 'choker' was generally superseded by a stiff narrow collar (see Fig. 82).

TROUSERS. The tight-fitting ankle-length breeches which had enjoyed such a long vogue were completely ousted in 1840 by the long, fairly full type of trousers fastened by a strap beneath the boot (see Plate XII, and Diagram Fig. 13), but the leg was cut tapering towards the foot. These trousers were comparatively close-fitting at the waist and foot, but much looser at the knee and down the leg. Greys and fawns were now considered more suitable than white or buff. About 1841 the front flap was abandoned, and trousers were made to button down the front, the buttons being hidden by an edging of the material.

Fig. 82. Day Dress 1852

Side-pockets also became general. During the forties, boot-straps were given up, and the trousers were allowed to flap loosely round the legs. From 1850 onwards trousers were frequently made of the same material as the coat (see Plate XIII, and Fig. 73), although large plaids and stripes were also worn with a coat of plain material (see Fig. 82). Another innovation of the fifties was the use of braid down the side of the trousers.

CLOTHES FOR THE YOUNG. A typical coat, waistcoat, and trousers for a youth of 1841 are shown in Fig. 83. The wide collar and cuffs should be noted also.

FOOTWEAR. Short *Wellington,* or *Reform, boots* were generally worn beneath the trousers until 1860, although a heavier lace-up boot came in during the fifties. Ordinary shoes were seldom worn. Low shoes with a buckle were worn at Court, and with a bow for evening wear.

Fig. 83. Youth 1841

Woolwork slippers for the home made their appearance during this period.

HEADGEAR. The favourite *top-hat* in its various forms still held the field in the forties (see Figs. 75, 76, 77, and 80). Many hats retained a tapered top and a large curled brim until 1855, but after that time the real straight *chimney-pot,* or *stove-pipe shape* with a narrow brim became general (see Figs. 78 and 79). Top-hats were made in black, white, or fawn. A short, flat, felt hat, with rather a straight brim, also came into favour in the fifties (see Fig. 73), but was chiefly used for travelling. Caps *with ear-flaps* also came into use for travelling, and a somewhat quaint sporting-cap is shown in Fig. 74. The tam-o'-shanter type of cap was still worn by youths in the early eighteen-forties (see Fig. 83). In the eighteen-fifties, however, it was superseded by a small round cap.

HAIRDRESSING. At the beginning of the reign the hair was still parted on one side, worn rather long, and waved. The face was generally clean-shaven (see Plate XII), with the exception of short *side-whiskers*, but occasionally a small *moustache* was worn (see Fig. 76). A small beard, known as the 'IMPERIAL' (see Figs. 71 and 128), a revival of the '*Royal*', in fashion during the seventeenth century, was worn in France during the Second Empire as a sign of adherence to the Bonaparte regime, and this fashion spread to other countries. During the fifties, the hair was cut somewhat shorter, moustaches were more general, and the side-whiskers were worn much longer except by very young men (see Fig. 82). It should be noted that the hair was usually well-oiled, and for this purpose a special variety of oil known as 'Macassar' was introduced by a Mr. Rowland in 1855. As everybody knows, chairs and sofas were in consequence festooned with antimacassars to prevent the hair-oil from staining the upholstery, and these articles became a fashionable adjunct from this date. Whiskers, descending the sides of the face in a narrow line, but widening under the chin, leaving the chin itself uncovered, were worn during the forties. His Royal Highness Prince Albert favoured whiskers of this type, which were in consequence much affected by young men of the period.

SMOKING. The habit of cigarette-smoking had been indulged in by the Spaniards during the eighteenth century. They made them by rolling the tobacco inside a piece of paper with their fingers. Spanish cigarette-cases of the eighteenth century were of silver, and cylindrical in form like modern shaving-soap cases. The cigarette was brought from Spain to France and to England. It became much more popular after the Crimean War (1856). The armies taking part in the campaign brought back the habit as the result of their fraternization with the Turks. Before that time, smoking was regarded with disfavour, and was only indulged in cautiously. After 1850 the habit of smoking cigars and cigarettes (pipes were only considered suitable to vulgar people) was looked upon as a refinement, probably owing to the fact that it had been adopted by some of the crowned heads of Europe. For instance, the Emperor Napoleon III, we are told in 1856, was very fond of smoking a 'few' cigarettes after luncheon and dinner.

The SMOKING JACKET was introduced into the masculine world of fashion at this time. It was considered genteel for the ladies to object strongly to the fumes of tobacco, so the gentlemen retired to another room, changing into a smoking jacket and often a cap while indulging in this 'noxious weed'. These jackets and caps were of velvet or some fancy silk, and often handsomely embroidered. When rejoining the ladies the ordinary coat replaced the smoking outfit and its inherent 'nasty smell'.

WOMEN'S COSTUME

A journal of the period informs its readers that 'On this 9th of November (1837), being Lord Mayor's Day, Her Majesty visited in State her liege city of London. The Sovereign of the World—for by that title may we call our Queen so long as "Britannia rules the waves" —graciously condescended to accept an invitation from her subjects to a banquet within the capital of her dominions; and with all the pomp belonging to Majesty, so went our blessed Queen Victoria within the city gates'.

On this propitious occasion the queen wore a costume of rich pink and silver brocade, the substance being of pink satin and the surface covered with silver in the closest embroidery, having lozenge-shaped spaces, in each of which was a full blown rose, with its leaves and buds in silver. The dress was of English manufacture. The Duchess of Sutherland (Mistress of the Robes), who rode in the same State carriage, wore a dress of blue and silver.

Queen Victoria opened her first Parliament on the twentieth of the same month in the same year.

'Her Majesty wore a white dress, presumably of satin, with a deep bullion fringe, a magnificent diadem of diamonds, ear-rings of diamonds, an ermine cape, a robe of crimson velvet and gold. The train was borne by Lord Kilmarnock, Master Ellice, and Master Cavendish, the Pages of Honour.' From another source we learn that this costume was further embellished with 'a superbly brilliant stomacher also of diamonds, and she wore a splendid diamond necklace'. During the latter part of the ceremony Her Majesty's train was borne by the Duchess of Sutherland and the Marchioness of Lansdowne on entering the House.

Much consternation was caused by the fact that as sovereign of the Most Noble Order of the Garter, Her Majesty would be expected to wear a Garter—but where? To ascertain the correct procedure was difficult. Reference to portraits of Queens Regnant were of no use. Queen Mary Tudor is not represented with the insignia in any portrait, as her husband, Philip, being joint sovereign, it was considered proper that they should be worn by him alone. No portrait of Queen Elizabeth shows her wearing the Garter. The same procedure applies to Queen

Mary II as to Queen Mary Tudor, William III being joint sovereign. Queen Anne wore the collar, George, and ribbon, but no Garter is seen in any of her portraits. This being so, a special embassy was sent to Ewelme, Oxfordshire, in 1837, to examine the effigy of Alice, Duchess of Suffolk (see 'Costume and Fashion', Vol. II, pp. 240 and 456). To the relief of all it was discovered that the duchess, a Lady of the Garter, was wearing the insignia buckled round her left forearm.[1] For some reason or other it was decided that Queen Victoria should wear her Garter high on the upper arm. It is seen worn in this manner in the portrait of the Queen by Winterhalter painted in 1845, and in another by the same artist painted in 1859. In later life, when Queen Victoria wore longer and wider sleeves, as shown in Fig. 180 (Chapter VI), the Garter was buckled on the forearm near the elbow.

The portrait by Sir George Hayter of Queen Victoria in her *Coronation Robes* taking the oath on her accession is well known. This ceremony formed part of her coronation 28th June 1838. A description of these regal robes here is appropriate.

Her dress was of white satin veiled with very beautiful lace. Over this was a garment equivalent to the dalmatic, open at the front and having large open sleeves. It was confined at the waist by a heavy gold girdle terminating in tassels. It was composed of cloth of gold woven with green palm branches from which sprang roses, shamrocks, and thistles in their natural colourings, and lined throughout with rose-coloured silk. Over the shoulders hung the armilla, or stole, of cloth of gold three inches in width embroidered with Tudor roses, shamrocks, and thistles, and silver eagles with Royal coronets between. At the ends were the arms of St. George, finished with a deep gold fringe and above the arms silver eagles.

The Imperial mantle, also of cloth of gold, was woven at Braintree, Essex. It took thirty yards of material. The pattern, brocaded on the gold cloth, was a scroll design in raised gold combining the red rose, green shamrock, and purple thistle; the whole garment being edged with gold bullion fringe two and a half inches deep and lined throughout with rose-coloured silk. The mantle was attached across the breast by a morse of gold ornamented with an eagle between two palm branches in the centre, and a rose, shamrock, and thistle at the sides. The crown used on this occasion may be seen at the Tower of London.

[1] This story was told to me by the late Earl of Oxford and Asquith in 1926. According to another account, Queen Victoria in simple naïveté asked of the Duke of Norfolk, 'My Lord Duke, where am I to wear the Garter?' Upon reference to various authorities *a print of Queen Anne* was found, in which it was seen that the Garter was placed on her left arm. I have not had the good fortune to find this print. (H. N.)

The *bridal dress* worn by Queen Victoria at her wedding in 1840 was entirely composed of white satin, with a close bodice, full skirt, and a long train worn separately. The lace flounce, three-quarters of a yard in depth, which trimmed the skirt, though properly called Honiton lace, was really worked at the village of Beer, ten miles from Honiton. More than two hundred persons were constantly employed upon it for more than nine months. The veil, a yard and a half square, was of the same lace, and fell from a coronal of orange blossoms. With this dress Her Majesty wore the Collar of the Garter.

In 1842, Queen Victoria gave her famous 'Plantagenet Ball' at Buckingham Palace, in which she appeared in a fourteenth-century costume worn over quantities of 1842 petticoats. Prince Albert represented King Edward III in gorgeous robes but with chin whiskers. Amongst many of the most aristocratic personages of this year was the Duchess of Beaufort as a Queen of Medieval Spain. Despite the fact that the celebrated J. R. Planché (1796–1880) was supposed to have supervised all the costumes, the modern corkscrew curls of the duchess were allowed to dangle beneath her richly bedizened medieval headdress.

A repetition of this ball was given at Stafford House in the following July.

During this period, and particularly in the forties, women's fashions, both in dress and coiffure, were much influenced by the costume of the reigns of Charles I and II (see Fig. 108).

A '*Stage Costume*' of the forties is shown in Fig. 84. Taking into consideration the archæological mentality of this time it is quite a commendable attempt at reproducing a Tudor dress. The drawing is made from a portrait by Chalon of Giulia Grisi in the character of 'Anne Boleyn'. Born at Milan she was the daughter of one of Napoleon's officers, and niece of Signora Grassini. Grisi made a great sensation as a *prima donna* during her sojourn in London from 1834 to 1854. In surveying Fig. 84 it is obvious that the fashions of the eighteen-forties influenced this historical costume, including the coiffure. The triangular tiara suggests the Gable headdress made so familiar by the portraits of Holbein. In the much be-pearled girdle one recognizes the origin of those gewgaws to be found in the glass cases of most theatrical costumiers. Giulia Grisi was the original 'Adalgisa' in Bellini's opera *Norma* and later became the wife of the Marchese di Candia (b. 1808, d. 1883) better known as that marvellous tenor Giuseppe Mario.

A greater artiste in costume was the French tragédienne, Élisa Rachel. Born 1820 she made her first stage appearance in 1837, and soon after became a member of the Comédie Française. She was chiefly famous for her interpretation of classical personages and created a furore by wearing clinging classic draperies at a time when immensely full skirts were the mode. Madame Pasta, the original 'Norma', had not possessed the artistic courage to flout contemporary fashion in this manner. Élisa Rachel visited London in 1841, St. Petersburg in

Fig. 84. 'Anne Boleyn' 1835

1853, and America in 1855. She died of consumption near Cannes in 1858.

The English actress, Fanny Kemble, who had gone to America in 1832, returned to London in 1840, but not to the stage. She had in the meantime married Pierce Butler, a wealthy American landowner and slave-owner. In 1840 she attended a reception at Stafford House given by the Duchess of Sutherland, at which Franz Liszt played and Rachel

recited. Fanny Kemble returned to the stage in 1847 and soon afterwards began the series of Shakespeare readings which really made her
famous. For these readings she wore contemporary costume, but
chose black velvet for the tragedies and white satin for the comedies.

Fig. 85. Négligé 1839   Fig. 86. Morning Dress 1839

She divorced her husband in 1848 on the ground of desertion, and
died in 1893.

One of the most important theatrical events of the nineteenth century
was the commencement of Charles Kean's management of the Princess's
Theatre in 1850. Here the talented son of Edmund Kean produced
Shakespeare in a lavish manner. Previous to his time no attempt
whatever was made to achieve correctness of costume or scenery.

Stage productions had considerably deteriorated in past years and slovenliness and shoddiness prevailed in most London theatres. Charles Kean set to work to reform all this, and he is rightly considered the pioneer of archæological productions.

Turning to ordinary clothes it should be noted that at the beginning

Fig. 87. Promenade Dress 1839

of Victoria's reign, the pointed *bodice* or *corsage* with a normal length of waist was general (see Figs. 87 and 88), although some dresses retained the waistband until the fifties (Fig. 86). In 1837, large sleeves gathered in at the wrist were still fashionable, and a full gauze oversleeve was sometimes worn with evening gowns. Very large sleeves, however, were disappearing, and by 1840 the sleeve was neatly gathered or tucked from the shoulders to the elbow, the fullness falling on the forearm and being gathered into a tight band at the wrist (see Plate XIV). The V-shaped front to the bodice was maintained by one or more collars tapering from the shoulders to the waist.

The MORNING DRESS shown in Fig. 85 consists of a *robe de chambre* in silk or satin, lined and turned back over the shoulders and down the

Fig. 88. Dinner Dress 1839

front, and fastened at the waist with a bow and long ends of ribbon. Large sleeves, widening to the wrist, are turned back revealing the full sleeve of the underdress. With this is worn a lace cap with ruchings of ribbon at the side, giving decided width.

Fig. 86 shows a *morning dress* in the form of a half-pelisse robe braided at the hem and up the left side terminating at the waistbelt. The sleeves are narrow on the upper arm and full from the elbow to the wristband.

A 'fashionable *public promenade dress*' is shown in Fig. 87. The pointed bodice has a cross-over 'berthe' of the same material and full bishop sleeves. The skirt has two flounces at the hem, and the upper skirt which is open at the front has a flounce at its edge.

The DINNER DRESS shown in Fig. 88 is very characteristic. The

Fig. 89. Walking Dress 1844

costume is in a light material, the skirt having two flounces of black lace headed by a twisted piping of a contrasting colour, the top flounce being caught up with a bow on the left side. The pointed bodice has a black lace berthe and wide, open elbow sleeves. An evening cap decorated with a cluster of flowers on each side and ribbons behind completes the ensemble. Black mittens are worn.

In the early forties, plain *sleeves*, fairly tight-fitting all the way down, became fashionable, and with some of these a small upper sleeve was worn. Fig. 89 is a *walking costume* carried out in a large check or plaid. The *bodice* was now as plain as possible, and the upper part

Fig. 90. Ball Dress 1846

was free of all the ornamentation which had served to exaggerate the breadth of the shoulders. Except for evening wear the bodice was now fairly high in the neck. A 'SEASIDE DRESS' of 1840 is described as having a 'corsage *en Amazone* of pink *poult de soie* trimmed with buttons, and a plain tight sleeve with lace cuff to match the fichu'. A white satin robe worn at the christening of the Princess Royal in 1841 had a 'corsage *à la corset* and short sleeves, the latter trimmed with Venetian mancherons of tulle edged with lace surmounted by a bouquet of short white ostrich-feathers attached by coques of lilac velvet ribbon'.

During the forties, a gathered *berthe* or *fichu* was sometimes worn with ball-gowns, and was so arranged as to leave the neck and shoulders quite bare (see Fig. 90). In 1844, a deep berthe of the same material as the bodice and skirt was often worn, and this variety was no longer V-shaped (see Plate XV). Another form of berthe was the '*cardinal pelerine*', worn longer at the back than in the front, and made of *point d'Angleterre* or other lace.

The 'Ladies' Cabinet' of 1845 contains a description of 'a white tarlatane robe over white *gros de Naples*, with a low round corsage, trimmed with a deep berthe of the same, beautifully embroidered, and short tight sleeves and volants worked to correspond'. Another evening dress of the same period had 'a low corsage, tight to the shape, and very deeply pointed at the bottom, with a row of lace standing up round the top, and a short sleeve rendered full by three festooned volants'.

At a concert in 1845, Queen Victoria is reported as wearing 'an elegant underdress of embroidered muslin, over this a round, open tunic richly embroidered and encircled with a frilling of rich lace of tasteful design, a high corsage, and short sleeves, frilled chemisette of white tulle, the entire dress lined with pale pink gauze giving it the appearance of a blush rose'.

There is an engraving of Her Majesty dated 1846 (Fig. 91), in which she wears a simple little white gown made on fashionable lines and a black silk scarf edged with fringe. The poke-bonnet surrounds the face, showing a lace frill next to the hair. It is trimmed with coloured ribbons and a light gauze veil.

The Queen was at all times anxious to support home industries, but this praiseworthy trait did not prevent her from ordering part of her wardrobe from Paris. Each year a consignment of dresses and bonnets was dispatched from that centre of fashion for her inspection. She was not, however, allowed an entirely free hand in this matter, as Prince Albert personally assisted in the choice of her apparel. In fact, he had very strong views on the subject of proper and becoming dress. This did not prevent Her Majesty from consulting him on every occasion—'his taste was always good'.

A fashion note of 1848 describes a costume worn by the Duchesse d'Orléans: 'Robe of black velvet, made perfectly plain, short loose elbow sleeves opening in the front to show the full undersleeve of white satin; the black sleeve being caught just at the bottom and finished with a row of white lace; low pelerine (or cape) to match, confined upon the centre with a fancy *nœud* of pink ribbon'.

COURT DRESS. A Court dress of 1848 is shown in Fig. 92.   The

Fig. 91. Queen Victoria 1846

sleeveless bodice is of velvet, and has a deep lace berthe worn very low and embellished with bows of ribbon at each shoulder.   The overskirt, complete with long train, is of the same material as the bodice, without any decoration, and is worn over an underskirt composed of a series of lace flounces mounted on satin.   It should be noted that the separate train which was a feature of the dress worn at Court during the reigns of George IV and William IV has given place to a train forming part of the dress itself in the fashion of the eighteenth century. The hair is parted in the centre, with spaniel curls at the sides, and drawn up into

Fig. 92. Court Dress 1848

a coil at the back. Numerous ostrich-plumes are worn, but lace lappets have gone out of use. Short gloves, pounced at the edges above the wrists, bracelets worn outside the gloves, and a long-sticked fan complete this ceremonial dress.

Queen Victoria introduced the custom of holding Drawing Rooms in the afternoon.   At 1.30 o'clock the doors of the State apartments were opened for the reception of the company.   Her Majesty generally entered the throne-room about three o'clock.

DRESS REFORM. In 1849, an ardent American reformer, Mrs. Amelia Bloomer, of Seneca Falls, Ohio, devised a new dress for women, con-

Fig. 93. Riding Habit 1855

sisting of a jacket with close sleeves, a skirt falling a little below the knee, and a pair of Turkish trousers.   She came to London in 1851 to propagate her views, but although a few extremists adopted the 'reformed dress', she did not meet with much response.   Leech cruelly ridiculed 'Bloomerism' in a series of cartoons in 'Punch', and the much-vaunted reform died a natural death.

RIDING HABITS. On equestrian expeditions Queen Victoria wore a

riding-habit, the body and sleeves of which were modelled on fashionable lines.   The skirt was of the usual amplitude.   Green was the
Queen's favourite colour for riding-habits, but she sometimes wore blue.
The costume was completed by a mannish top-hat in beaver, as shown
in Fig. 64 (Chapter III), with or without a veil, at other times by a

Fig. 94. Afternoon Gown 1852

cloth peaked cap as worn by the boys in Figs. 43 and 83, but with
a deeper gold border like that in Fig. 37.
    A smart riding-habit of the year 1855 (Fig. 93) is carried out in blue
cloth, the jacket trimmed with sealskin and finished at the neck with
an embroidered white collar.   The rather wide sleeves are short enough
to show full white undersleeves diving into buff gauntlet gloves.   The
lady of the fashion-plate lifts her skirt to show a white, embroidered

petticoat. This seems somewhat strange, as we know that riding trousers were worn beneath the habit at this time. The hat is a low-crowned close beaver, ornamented with a black ribbon bow and black *coque* feathers. The equestrian bronze statue of Queen Victoria at Liverpool shows her similarly attired, with the addition of the Garter ribbon.

A young lady when riding in the park (or elsewhere) was always accompanied by a groom in attendance, and woe betide her if she rode alone. She would be considered to have outraged the rules of Victorian propriety. She was harshly treated, perhaps, but the Society of the time would stand no tampering with social conventions.

Fig. 94 is an example of an *outdoor costume* of 1852. It is made in taffeta, the close-fitting bodice having a turn-down collar and an exaggerated form of bell-sleeve over a full lawn undersleeve. The sleeves and skirt are trimmed with numerous bands of the same material as the dress, pinked at the edges and laid on flat, with a single band of ruching set between them as shown in the drawing. The long ribbon ends depending from the bow at the waist are also ruched.

Queen Victoria in sports costume is shown in Fig. 95, taken from a picture by Landseer. The costume is probably made of Scotch home-spun, decorated with braid, and the bodice has a basque. In the picture the Queen appears to have removed the cloak of the same material from her shoulders and fastened it round her waist.

Balmoral Castle was purchased by the Queen in 1852 and was rebuilt from plans made by Prince Albert. Osborne House had already been acquired in 1840, and this was rebuilt from the prince's plans. His Royal Highness also designed the 'Balmoral Tartan', a mixture of red and grey. The Queen was not to be outshone, so designed one for herself in the same colours but introducing a white stripe. This was known as the 'Victoria Tartan'. Queen Victoria, a descendant from that picturesque, but unfortunate family, the Stuarts, was herself an ardent Jacobite. This family enthusiasm was carried to such an extreme that Her Majesty made the Stuart Tartan the dominant note in the decoration and furnishing of Balmoral. Curtains, wall coverings, and furniture coverings were all of the white Royal Tartan, and even the carpets were woven *en suite*. This Scottish influence spread to costume and inaugurated a craze for having dresses and dress-trimmings made of tartans.

The *wedding dress* of the Empress Eugénie is illustrated in Fig. 96, from a contemporary engraving. Eugénie Marie, Comtesse de Montijo, became Empress of the French on her marriage to Napoleon III at

Notre-Dame on the 30th January 1853.   An eyewitness stated that at this ceremony Eugénie in 'her dress of white uncut velvet and lace was perfection'.   The ornaments on her bodice and sleeves were sapphires surrounded with diamonds.   Her diadem was of diamonds and sapphires, wreathed with orange blossoms.   At the civil marriage in the Salle des

Fig. 95. Queen Victoria 1853

Marécheaux at the Tuileries, the empress wore a rose-coloured satin dress, with a rich garniture of lace and a circlet of gold and diamonds. It is said that the Empress Eugénie sought to revive the refined glories of the Court of Marie Antoinette, but the Court of the Second Empire, though decidedly chic, never achieved the artistic graces of Versailles.

At a public ceremony attended by the Empress in 1855, the skirt of her magnificent cherry-coloured velvet dress was entirely covered with

Alençon lace valued at twenty-five thousand francs. In this year, Worth introduced his MANTEAU DE COUR. This court mantle or train hung from the shoulders, instead of the waist, a radical departure from previous custom. It immediately became the Royal

Fig. 96. The Empress Eugénie 1853

fashion and the Empress wore one of *moiré antique* embroidered with gold.

SLEEVES. The tight-fitting sleeve was still in use with morning and afternoon dresses as late as 1855, but fashion throughout this reign was extremely varied, and a *bell-shaped sleeve* which first appeared about 1844 was occasionally worn during the late forties (see Fig. 97), and became general in the fifties (see Fig. 98, and Plate XVI). These bell-shaped sleeves were generally worn over a tight *undersleeve* or a full lawn sleeve gathered at the wrist. The undersleeve was sometimes made of fine batiste covered with embroidery. Another variety of

Fig. 97. Afternoon Gown 1848

sleeve in use about 1848 was of a plain, full, square shape, open up the side and generally trimmed with wide braid. With the wide open sleeve full undersleeves of lace, or embroidered lawn or muslin, were usually worn. These were known as '*false sleeves*' because they reached only just above the elbow where they were tied or fixed with an elastic band. At the wrist they were finished off with a frill or flounce of lace.

BODICES in the late forties and throughout the fifties were generally tight-fitting and high in the neck, being often cut into small tabs at the waist. A close-fitting *jacket* with tight sleeves was also in vogue in the fifties. Some of these jackets were finely embroidered in the style of the eighteenth century, and cut away short at the back (see Fig. 99). ZOUAVE JACKETS were also occasionally worn in the

Fig. 98. Indoor Dress 1857

forties. Blouse-like *chemisettes* of batiste and lace were another variation worn under bodices of silk or wool. They were sometimes called '*canezous*'.

COLLARS AND NECKWEAR. Collars were generally in keeping with the sleeves. At the beginning of the reign, broad collars were worn to correspond with the large full sleeves (see Plate XIV), whilst a narrower collar came in with the tight-fitting sleeve. Both varieties were usually of lace or finely embroidered batiste in white or beige (see Fig. 98). Neck ornaments for evening wear decreased in popularity. The neck and shoulders were usually left quite bare, the only article of jewellery being a simple brooch pinned on the top of the corsage.

CLOAKS AND MANTLES. At the end of the thirties, the *cloak* or *wrap*

Fig. 99. Outdoor Dress 1855

was still fashionable. It was worn ankle length, circular in shape, and had a fairly large overcape. In winter it was padded inside and trimmed with fur. Other *mantles* of a heavy character were decorated with braided designs. Shot-silk *capes* with long pointed fronts, often heavily fringed, were also worn. About 1840, sleeve-holes were made in the wrap, through which the arms could be passed, and sometimes wide sleeves were added. This gave the wrap a more cloak-like character,

which was emphasized by the omission of the overcape and the addition
of a hood.

Fig. 100 shows a *pelisse cloak* worn over a plaid dress. The pelisse
is moulded to the shoulders, and ornamented with braid and a lace

Fig. 100. Carriage Dress 1839

collar.   It is drawn in to the waist by a cord and tassels, and descends
nearly full length.   The full hanging sleeves are gathered in to the
shoulders, and have a perpendicular slit edged with braid through which
the hand passes.

A 'BURNOUS MANTLE' for evening wear is shown in Fig. 101.
It has the usual burnous hood, is ornamented in front with frogs and
tassels, and fastens from the V-neck to the waist.   It is lined with

plaid silk and edged with deep fringe. For back arrangement of burnous see Fig. 153 (1860).

A mantle, having its origin in the folded cornerwise shawl, known as the *pelerine* was fashionable from about 1837 to 1844. It was a short

Fig. 101. Burnous Mantle 1839

cape, the sides continuing in long ends which fell down the centre of the gown. Usually made of silk, it had one or more frills of the same material round its edge, but not down the fronts. In 1844 the pelerine was called a '*Mantelet écharpe*' (or *scarf mantle*).

About 1850 the majority of *wraps* were worn shorter and not so thickly padded (see Fig. 102). They were now made of lighter materials, mostly silk, and trimmed with ruching round the sleeves and border.

COLOUR ILLUSTRATIONS

PLATE I. 1800 (*see* pp. 7, 11, 14, & 49)

PLATE II. 1810 (*see* pp. 9–11 & 14)

PLATE III. 1820 (Frontispiece; *see also* pp. 10, 12, & 49)

PLATE IV. 1800 (*see* pp. 18 & 36)

PLATE V. 1810 (*see* pp. 22, 28, & 36)

PLATE VI. 1820 (*see* pp. 26, 33–4, & 35)

PLATE VII. 1830 (*see* pp. 44–5 & 49)

PLATE VIII. 1827 (*see* pp. 54, 59, & 80)

PLATE IX. 1837 (*see* pp. 70–1, 79, & 81)

PLATE X. 1833 (*see* pp. 71 & 77–80)

PLATE XI. 1837 (*see* pp. 77, 78, & 80)

PLATE XII. 1840 (*see* pp. 89, 95, & 98)

PLATE XIII. 1850 (*see* pp. 89 & 94–6)

PLATE XIV. 1840 (*see* pp. 105 & 117)

PLATE XV. 1844 (*see* pp. 108, 123, & 131)

PLATE XVI. 1856 (*see* pp. 116, 122, 126, 130, & 132)

PLATE XVII. 1860 (*see* pp. 136, 139, 140, 142, & 146)

PLATE XVIII. 1870 (*see* pp. 137, 142, & 146)

PLATE XIX. 1860 (*see* pp. 152, 191, & 193)

PLATE XX. 1870 (*see* pp. 170–1 & 192)

PLATE XXI. 1880
(*see* pp. 199, 201, & 204)

PLATE XXII. 1892
(*see* pp. 199 & 201–4)

PLATE XXIII. 1900 (*see* pp. 200–2 & 204)

PLATE XXIV. 1878 (*see* pp. 178, 208, 210, & 246)

PLATE XXV. 1888 (*see* pp. 208, 224, & 245)

PLATE XXVI. 1895 (*see* pp. 208–9, 230, & 247)

PLATE XXVII. 1900 (*see* pp. 208, 237, & 246–7)

Winter wraps were made of fine cloth or velvet.   Lighter capes were also in use with trimmings of fringe or passementerie.

The ' Ladies' Cabinet' of 1845 shows a variety of capes and mantles.

Fig. 102. Walking Dress 1850

A detailed description is given of a puce-coloured velvet 'mantelet' for 'morning visiting'.

The front of the corsage fits closely to the bust, the back descends in the pelerine form nearly to the level of the knee, but it is sloped out at the bend of the arm and bordered with velvet lace, two flounces of which surmount the bottom one; the upper part of the corsage is trimmed with a single volant placed horizontally, and the long scarf ends are decorated from top to bottom with a row of passementerie in the centre and two deep volants horizontally.

The same journal describes the 'Casimir cloak, three-quarter length, made loose from the shoulders, with a pelerine of an extremely large size, and long, moderately wide sleeves; a fur collar confines the cloak at the throat, and a broad band of fur encircles the round of the cloak, the pelerine, and the bottom of the sleeves'. The black lace 'mantelet à la Reine' was much in vogue in 1845, and the 'Ladies' Cabinet' also describes 'a black filet de soie mantelet trimmed with black lace'. This variety of mantle was also worn in 1856 (see Plate XVI). Another characteristic mode of that year was the 'burnous à la bédouin', or Arab cloak.

Paisley shawls and Cashmere scarves were much worn with 'walking-dresses' throughout this period. For evening wear, black lace shawls, folded cornerwise to give a triangular shape, and sometimes large enough to cover the whole dress, were very modish. Fur boas continued in fashion until 1840.

MATERIALS. Two of the most popular materials for dresses during the forties were barége (a French gauze) and organdie muslin. In the fifties a figured silk called broché was very fashionable, as well as bombazine, a light woollen fabric crossed with cotton. Woollen fabrics began to be made in France during the fifties.

Jet trimming was introduced in 1855. There was a revival of interest in lace about this time, and lace-making was reintroduced in France.

An aniline dye which produced a brilliant violet colour was introduced in 1856, and, in consequence of this, violet became an extremely fashionable colour.

The glories of the Great Exhibition of 1851 set all tongues in Her Majesty's dominions wagging. The exhibition also started a craze for machine-made materials, much to the chagrin of the hand-loom weavers.

The first sewing-machine was brought to London in 1844. Its inventor was a Parisian named Barthélemy Thinonnier. During the revolution of July 1830, when Charles X lost his throne, the tailors and seamstresses, fearing that this innovation would add to the number of the unemployed, smashed up all the available sewing-machines. The unfortunate Thinonnier was left with only one, his original model, which he took with him to England. Some sewing-machines were in use in England in the early fifties. The inventor died of a broken heart and insolvent in the year 1857.

SKIRTS. At the beginning of the reign, skirts were long and very full and were worn over drill petticoats set out with stiff flounces and even whalebones. In the forties full petticoats of woven horsehair were introduced. The bell-shaped skirt itself was sometimes ornamented with a wide flounce (see Fig. 103), and ball-dresses had one or two flounces and loopings of flowers (see Fig. 90). Morning and promenade dresses were made of tartans and spotted foulards as well as plain materials (see Figs. 89 and 103). During the forties, a number of dresses were enriched with fine gold thread, whilst others were elaborately or delicately embroidered with coloured silks (see Plate XV).

The 'Ladies' Cabinet' of 1845 has a description of a dress of white

Fig. 103. Promenade Dress 1842

gros de Naples, with a *double skirt*, the upper one descending considerably below the knee, both being embroidered round the border. The same journal draws attention to a 'home dress' of green foulard, 'the skirt trimmed very high with *flounces*, placed five, four, and three together, each portion being placed at some distance from the other . A 'home dinner dress' in pale lavender 'poult de soie' is also described;

'the skirt is trimmed high with flounces put three together; they are deep, laid on in light festoons, and each portion headed by a *rouleau* (or *piped trimming*)'.

In 1850 a watch-pocket was frequently inserted at the waist-line of the skirt.

Skirts grew longer year by year, entirely concealing the feet, and, in addition to being worn over several petticoats, were sometimes padded at the hips or at the back.   The full bell-shaped skirt continued throughout the fifties, which also witnessed the introduction of the CRINOLINE. This was revived in France by the Empress Eugénie in 1855, and not,

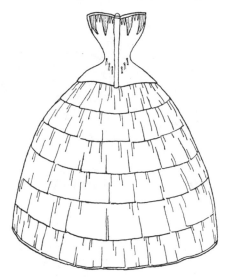

Fig. 104. Crinoline Petticoat 1855

as sometimes supposed, invented by her.   It was but a copy of the sixteenth-century farthingale, its further development echoing the eighteenth-century hoop and panier.   Its name is derived from the horsehair cloth of which petticoats had lately been made, the component parts of which were hair (Latin *crinis*) and thread (*linum*).   The 'crinoline' was a petticoat into which bands of whalebone or steel were inserted horizontally.   These bands increased in size as they descended towards the feet.   The *crinoline petticoat* is depicted in Fig. 104, which also shows the corset extending well on to the hips. Shortly after its appearance in France, the crinoline was introduced into England, and, although furiously attacked from time to time, it was soon universally worn.   During its long career, the crinoline passed through many changes, all involving an increase in size and circumference. At first the crinoline was slightly held back from the front by ties, but after a while it became more nearly circular in shape, only to recede again in front in the late sixties.

Fig. 105. The Empress Eugénie 1855

The great width of the skirt led to an increasing lavishness of *trimming*. Dresses were often worn with several flounces, either of the same material as the skirt or of print or embroidered braid, each flounce overlapping the one beneath. Sometimes, instead of flounces, the skirts themselves were worn in tiers, elaborately embroidered (see Fig. 99). Other dresses were made of vertical strips of alternating materials sewn together, and widening from the waist downwards (see Plate XVI). The introduction of the crinoline, in fact, gave the dress-designers free scope for the exercise of their most extravagant fancies. Some really charming examples of crinoline dresses are to be found in the drawings of Gavarni, and in 1856 the Empress Eugénie is described as wearing a costume designed by him.

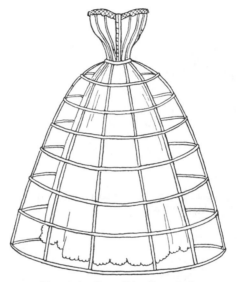

Fig. 106. Cage Crinoline 1856

Fig. 105 is a drawing made from a portrait of the empress by Winterhalter at Versailles. The dress is of white satin with two flounces of deep white lace, and is devoid of any other trimming except diamonds. The court train of green velvet is long and wide and fastened on at the back of the waist. It is bordered with gold lace, edged with a rouleau of cloth of gold, and lined with white satin. The well-known coronet of the Empress is worn, with a small veil hanging from it. Her decoration is the ribbon of the Legion of Honour.

We are told that the Empress changed her clothes frequently, hardly ever wearing the same dress more than twice. The amplitude of her skirts was simply fabulous, 'all this stuff being supported by a sort of skeleton of an extremely flexible iron'. This type of *crinoline* or *cage* was composed entirely of narrow bands of steel descending perpendicularly from the waist, crossed by other bands at right angles forming the circumference. (See Fig. 106 with contemporary corset.) One frequently finds this form of crinoline ridiculed by 'Mr. Punch'. Not only was this contrivance very inconvenient, *but some even saw so far as to consider it indecent.* A contemporary writer bitterly complains that 'there is no hope for us while dress is so hideous, while the senseless crinoline is worn'.

A member of the French Court informs us that

the Empress is greatly attached to this cage, which to us seems very ungraceful and inconvenient. She sticks to it in spite of the quips of the Emperor, to whom she simply replies that she does not know how she lived so many years without a cage. I can only find two excuses for this fashion. One is that women who wear it have their legs free in walking, and are not hampered by skirts and petticoats hanging on their calves and thighs and hampering their movements; the other, in her case, is that there is a sort of harmony between the amplitude of the woman and the size of the apartments in which she lives. In our little rooms, to get through our narrow doors, walking in the street and on the pavement, such a thing is as absurd as it is inconvenient. But in these great, lofty apartments, a slight woman in tight-fitting garments would be lost, would seem of no consequence. Here a dozen women adorn the salon admirably, and are in harmony with the wide spaces, the ample seats, the width and height of the doors.

The Empress Eugénie has always been credited with excellent taste; but the following excerpt from a letter dated July 23rd 1856 gives one furiously to think: 'the Empress came in wearing a floating robe of garnet colour or thereabouts, with a number of cross-bands of green and yellow, and an ample crinoline'.

UNDERCLOTHES. During Victoria's reign, there seems to have been a strong tendency for women to clothe themselves as warmly as possible. Five or six *petticoats* were worn, both before and after the introduction of the crinoline. The underneath one was generally of red or white flannel, but in very cold weather was made of padded silk. Then came several petticoats of strong coloured material trimmed with braid, or starched white petticoats with stiff flounces. Ladies of fashion sometimes made use of silk and cotton, or white embroidered materials. During the forties, full petticoats of a new kind were introduced. They were made of a material woven from hair which was known as 'crinoline'. It was not until 1855, when bands of cane or steel were inserted in the petticoat, that the article of clothing itself took the name of crinoline. Except for evening wear, a high *chemise* was worn with sleeves reaching to the elbow. During the thirties and forties, long, stiffly whaleboned *corsets* were indispensable to achieve the fashionable wasp-waist, but in the fifties shorter corsets were worn to reveal the natural curves of the upper part of the bust (see Figs. 104 and 106).

Long-legged *drawers*, with or without lace trimmings, were universally worn, and white *stockings* were usually favoured.   Towards the end of this period, drawers were frequently known as '*bloomers*', although they bore little resemblance to the pseudo-Oriental trousers designed for women's wear by the celebrated Mrs. Amelia Bloomer of Ohio.

In the fifties stockings with wide horizontal stripes were frequently worn.   These stockings had a white ground, the stripes usually matching the colour of the dress.

FOOTWEAR. Shoes of the heelless sandal type were retained for indoor wear, but after 1840 most outdoor shoes had low heels and large rosettes.   Boots reaching just above the ankle and laced up the inner side, with rather square toes, were also worn.   From 1850 onwards, boots with elastic sides were frequently in use.   Both boots and shoes were made of satin, kid, or coloured silk.

An amusing anecdote is told of the Empress Eugénie.   Upon one occasion at a State concert where she was enforced to sit for a considerable while, she was much troubled by the tightness of her very small shoes.   Nothing daunted, she slipped them off and kicked them under her chair.   When the time came for her to make a graceful exit, the shoes could not be found, and it was only after a thorough search that they were discovered some distance from where she had been sitting.

HEADDRESSES. There was an endless variety of hats and bonnets worn during this period, and indeed throughout the whole of Victoria's long reign.   The *poke bonnet* in various forms continued from the preceding reign, but the large, flat, circular hat had gone completely out of fashion.   A fashion journal of 1840 describes a 'white figured silk bonnet, a round shape, the interior trimmed with flowers, the exterior with figured ribbon and a white willow plume, and a lace *voilette* (or *veil*) at the edge of the brim completes the trimming'. This confection was recommended for seaside wear.   A straw bonnet with a straight poke front (see Fig. 97), was much favoured until 1850, when the front was considerably reduced in size and made to fit more closely round the face.   The larger-brimmed bonnet had a little frill by the ears (see Figs. 97 and 103), and the tight-brimmed bonnet often had a frill all round the back and sides (see Fig. 94).   These frills on the bonnet were called '*bavolets*'.   In nearly every case the bonnet was secured by long ribbons tied in a bow under the chin.   Sometimes these ribbons, which were called '*brides*', were worn untied and allowed to hang down on either side of the face.   Flowers were much used for trimming both the interior and exterior of the bonnet.   Ostrich feathers were often used as trimmings, and sometimes a large floating veil was allowed to hang freely from the back of the crown (see Fig. 103).

A close-fitting form of hat or bonnet called the 'CAPOTE' was much in favour during the forties. The 'Ladies' Cabinet' of 1845 describes 'a capote of yellow crape *bouillonné*, a round and rather large shape, the exterior decorated with ribbon to correspond and two roses with a gerbe of foliage placed on one side, the interior decorated with coques of ribbon', and also a '*capote Clarisse* of dark coloured satin lined with

Fig. 107. Cap 1837

blue velvet, the interior trimmed with coques of velvet ribbon, brides *en suite*, the exterior with a long drooping feather and ribbon both corresponding with the satin'. The same guide to fashion mentions 'an *Italian straw chapeau*, a small round shape trimmed with a wreath of wild flowers to which floating brides of green ribbon are attached'.

Queen Victoria is described in 1845 as wearing a 'bonnet of white chip, rounded and rather low at the ears, the crown entirely concealed by a splendid long ostrich feather slightly curled at the tip, and with brides of rich white ribbon tied under the centre of the chin',

In the fifties, a large flat *mushroom hat* in leghorn was a characteristic feature, (see Fig. 99). The small crown was usually encircled by a wreath of flowers, and fairly wide ribbons decorated both the interior and exterior of the hat. This style was mostly favoured by girls and young women, the older generation remaining faithful to the close-fitting bonnet. Even comparatively young women, however, sometimes preferred a smart Parisian bonnet of the type shown in Plate XVI.

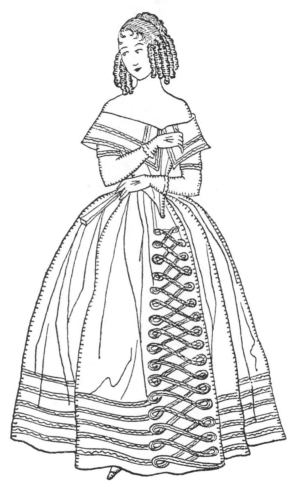

Fig. 108. Evening Dress 1842

For indoor wear, small *lace caps*, trimmed in a simple style with satin or velvet ribbon, were extremely popular (see Fig. 85). Other caps were made of embroidered muslin, trimmed with Mechlin or other lace. The Duchesse d'Orléans is described in 1848 as wearing a cap of white lace adorned with pink flowers. During the fifties, married women invariably wore a cap or bonnet in the house. A wreath of flowers was often worn instead of a cap with evening dress. A typical *evening cap* is shown in Fig. 88.

MOURNING. Fig. 107 shows a cap of the late thirties. It was made entirely of plain white stiffened muslin. When decorated with flowers and coloured ribbon it was fashionable for indoor wear, but this style when unrelieved by any colour was worn by widows in conjunction with a turned-down white muslin collar and cuffs.

There is a portrait of Queen Adelaide, dated 1840, wearing widow's weeds. The cap of plain white muslin is similar to that shown in Fig. 107, but the collar has two goffered frills of muslin, and the cuffs of the same material, at least eight inches in depth, have an opaque hem two and a half inches deep top and bottom, showing three inches of transparent muslin in between. The dress in plain black silk is modelled on fashionable lines.

HAIRDRESSING. The exaggerated loops and puffs of hair in vogue in the preceding reign had completely gone out of fashion. The hair was now parted in the centre and tightened in a top setting of plaits, with pendant (or 'spaniel') curls over the ears (see Figs. 89 and 108). Sometimes the side-curls were dispensed with, and the flat, parted hair was brought in a curved shape to the front of the ears (see Plate XV), or in a small plait allowing the ear to show, or in a plaited knot at either side. There were in fact several varieties of hairdressing in use during the forties. The front hair was frequently disposed in soft bands at the sides and the back hair in plaited braids arranged in the style of a coronet round the summit of the head. Another coiffure consisted of a profusion of ringlets at the sides and a full knot at the back of the head. Sometimes the hair was decorated with a band of ribbon at the back and a butterfly bow at the side. For evening wear a wreath of flowers was often worn, or a single flower at one side, preferably a camellia (see Fig. 90). From 1850 onwards, the hair was waved, parted in the centre, and simply curved from the forehead over the ears in a fuller manner, sometimes being turned under to increase the fullness at the sides, whilst the back hair was arranged lower down on the nape of the neck (see Fig. 98).

GLOVES and MITTENS, both long and short, were in use, the mittens being frequently embroidered in the French style. Broad BRACELETS were much in vogue, especially with ball dresses. MUFFS of smaller dimensions than heretofore were always fashionable in winter. HAND-BAGS were generally carried, and were made of silk or velvet decorated with bullion, beads, sequins, braid, or needlework. They were often set in elaborate silver, steel, or gilt mounts. FANS and small BOUQUETS or posies were usually indispensable adjuncts of the ball dress. Fans were a little longer in the stick than previously. PARASOLS were still small and of various shapes and materials, sometimes heavily fringed, and sometimes made of lace and decorated with a large ribbon bow (see Plate XVI). Sometimes the stick of the parasol was jointed in the middle, so that the complexion of the holder might be protected from the sun at any angle. Tiny parasols were even affixed to carriage-whips for use when driving.

LIST OF ARTISTS WORKING AT THIS PERIOD

Eugène Louis Lami	1800–1890
Paul Gavarni	1801–1866
George Baxter	1804–1867
Franz Xavier Winterhaller	1806–1873
John Leech	1818–1864

The Pre-Raphaelite Movement came into being in 1850. The prime movers were:

Ford Madox Brown	1821–1893
William Holman Hunt	1827–1910
Dante Gabriel Rossetti	1828–1882
John Everett Millais	1829–1896
William Morris	1834–1896

CHAPTER V

MID-VICTORIAN PERIOD (1857–77)

CONTEMPORARY FOREIGN GOVERNMENTS

FRANCE: The Second Empire, Napoleon III (1852–70)
          The Third Republic (1870 onwards)
PRUSSIA: Frederick William IV (1840–61)
          William I (1861–88)
GERMAN EMPIRE: William I (1871–88)
AUSTRIA: Francis Joseph (1848–1916)
RUSSIA: Alexander II (1855–81)
SPAIN: Isabella II (1833–70)
          Amadeo I (1870–73)
          Republic (1873–74)
          Alphonso XII (1874–86)
ITALY: Victor Emmanuel II (1861–78)

INTRODUCTION

THE domestic life of the royal family was everything that could be desired, and we have it on the authority of Her Majesty's letters that she and her husband were supremely happy.   There is an old saying that 'Peace, Happiness, and Prosperity reign when a woman occupies the throne, since men rule the kingdom', and this was fully true at this period.   In addition to being indispensable to the happiness of the Queen, Prince Albert devoted himself and his whole life to the welfare of the Queen's subjects.   In everything but the title he was the King of Great Britain, but Her Majesty, doubtful whether the nation sufficiently appreciated the excellent qualities of her husabnd, and in order to increase his prestige, in June 1857 created him Prince Consort.

The high moral example set by the Queen and the Prince Consort had a tremendous influence on the propriety and decorum of the nation in general, and particularly on the Society of the day—usually referred to as High Life at this time—as it was commonly recognized that any breach of the moral code would entail the complete loss of Royal favour, and consequent banishment from Court circles.   It does not follow that moral lapses and peccadilloes did not take place, but any breach of the 'eleventh commandment' spelt ruin for the culprits.

Although the Matrimonial Causes Act passed in 1857 removed many of the obstacles to obtaining a severance of irksome connubial ties, the Royal pair, and particularly the Sovereign herself, set their faces rigidly against any taint of the divorce court, and any one having made an appearance in that court forfeited all hope of ever again appearing at Royal functions. Her Majesty carried her veneration of the sanctity of the holy state of matrimony to such a point that she could not find it right or proper that a widow should marry again.

From 1854 to 1856 Her Majesty's forces were engaged in the Crimean War, and hardly had the echoes of that sordid campaign died away when the storm which had been brewing in India for some time, broke in all the appalling horrors of the Mutiny, which lasted from 1857 to 1859. During this rebellion 'khaki' was used, having made its first appearance in India as early as 1849.

The year 1861 brought bitter grief to Her Majesty. Early in that year her mother—the Duchess of Kent—died; but far worse was to follow as the year drew to its close. Inclement weather during a visit of the Prince Consort to Sandhurst afflicted him with a chill, and he had hardly recovered from this, when a flying visit to Cambridge to see the Prince of Wales brought on a relapse from which he never recovered. Ill as he was, he did not relax his efforts for peace in the world, and his emendation of a dispatch on the American question, which in its original form would have dragged the country into a war with the United States, occupied much of his time during the last days of his illness. On 14th December 1861 this noble spirit passed to his rest, and with him went all the joy of life, so far as Queen Victoria was concerned.

For ten years, to the sorrow and chagrin of her subjects, the Queen was, with few exceptions, seldom seen in public, and the effects of the Queen's great dole were heavily felt throughout the kingdom. Her protracted mourning engendered a morbid abasement to grief amongst her people, so that costly and ostentatious funerals became the order of the day. These became magnificent entertainments, indulged in by all classes of the community; the custom has survived only among the lower orders, who, to this day, keep up the custom of elaborate burial, and thoroughly enjoy a well-managed interment.

The public interest taken in the Great Exhibition of 1851 stimulated the idea of a second. The International Exhibition of 1862 was held in a special building erected to the design of Captain Fowke with a frontage in Cromwell Road, Kensington. The original Exhibition buildings of 1851 in Hyde Park were removed and re-erected at Sydenham in 1854, where, to this day, they are known to all the world as the Crystal Palace.

A very bright spot in the gloom which submerged the Royal Court was the marriage of Albert Edward, Prince of Wales, to the beautiful Danish princess, Alexandra, which took place at Windsor on 10th March 1863. 'The Queen did not intrude her widow's robes into the joyful ceremony, but watched it from her closet near the altar.' In exuberant and enthusiastic welcome the British public took the new Princess of Wales to its heart, and never, till her death in 1925, as Princess, Queen, or Queen Mother, did she ever lose her place in its affections. Henceforward their Royal Highnesses fulfilled all functions appertaining to the Sovereign in the absence of Her Majesty the Queen.

In February 1866, after some pressure had been brought to bear, Her Majesty consented to open Parliament, but with absence of full State. This ceremony was repeated the following year, though on neither occasion did the Queen read the Address to Parliament.

In November 1868 the end of the Shogun dynasty in Japan, through revolution, produced a reformed government, at the head of which was placed the Mikado. This is a matter of some sartorial interest, as the Japanese, in their zeal for progress, abandoned to some extent their quaint and highly artistic garb, adopting in its place the horrible and thoroughly unsuitable garments of the Western civilization.

The Suez Canal, opening out the East to the West, was completed in 1869. On 17th November of that year the canal was formally opened in great State in the presence of the Emperor of Austria, the Emperor and Empress of the French, the Khedive, and the Crown Prince of Prussia.

War between France and Germany was declared on 14th July 1870. The Battle of Sedan, 1st September, sealed the fate of the Second French Empire, when the Emperor surrendered to the King of Prussia, the Empress fled to England, and the Prince Imperial (b. 1856; assegaied in Zululand 1879) to Belgium.

The period following the Franco-German War of 1870 was a dull one from a sartorial point of view; and it was not until the advent of Marshal MacMahon as President that Paris recovered anything like her former brilliancy. During the MacMahon administration, not only the *Salons* and receptions returned to the magnificence of the Empire, but the Races regained their splendour and became veritable fashion shows.[1]

The Education Act, passed in 1870, gave a tremendous fillip to the

[1] Marshal MacMahon was elected President May 25th 1873 and retired Jan. 1879.

democratic system. Concurrent with this, the adoption of machinery, replacing to a great extent skilled manual labour, in factories and work-shops, had the lamentable result of practically wiping out the older type of craftsmen, men who did their work thoroughly and conscientiously, creating those masterpieces of the arts which did much to make England of the past so beautiful.

The uninterrupted retirement of the Sovereign gradually produced a feeling of discontent and disappointment amongst the populace; a decided leaning towards republicanism was rife, which reached its climax in 1871. To conciliate her subjects, the Queen, now a middle-aged woman of fifty-two, was induced to take part again in the ceremonial of the realm. In 1876 Disraeli introduced the Bill whereby Queen Victoria added the title of Empress of India to that of Queen of Great Britain. Considerable opposition was encountered to the addition, but it was considered to be advisable in view of the assumption of the Government of India by the Crown. The Queen was much gratified by the passing of the Bill, and signified her pleasure by creating Disraeli Earl of Beaconsfield. In the following January Her Majesty was proclaimed Empress at the Imperial Durbar which was held at Delhi.

Her Imperial Majesty opened the fourth session of her ninth Parliament in person in February 1877, and in the following April held a Drawing Room at St. James's Palace.

During this period the country was embroiled in war with Afghanistan from 1868 to 1878.

At no period in the history of costume have the clothes of men and women been so supremely hideous as those generally worn during the sixties and early seventies of the nineteenth century.

MEN'S COSTUME

THE COAT OR JACKET. Throughout the whole of this period, a short, single-breasted coat or jacket reaching to the middle of the thigh was much in evidence, both as part of a complete suit or with trousers of a different material (see Fig. 109, and Plate XVII). This jacket was usually square-cut, although in the seventies it was often slightly rounded in front. The collar was sometimes cut in a small V-shape at the neck with narrow lapels, and sometimes buttoned right up to the neck with no lapels at all (see Plate XVII). Pocket-flaps were reduced in size, and a breast-pocket was often placed on the left side of the coat.

This form of jacket was also used for shooting and other field sports (see Plate XVIII).

A variety of single-breasted *morning coats* were also worn, with a narrow collar and lapels, and rounded-off fronts to the skirts (see Fig. 110). Both jacket and morning-coat were usually worn buttoned up at the

Fig. 109. Outdoor Dress 1870   Fig. 110. Walking Dress 1865

neck, the lower buttons being left undone to show the lower part of the waistcoat.

The double-breasted *frock coat* with a moderately tight waist was still in favour, but the lapels had decreased in depth and velvet collars were no longer worn (see Fig. 111). The Prince of Wales is shown in Fig. 112 (taken from a contemporary photograph), wearing a black frock coat of the period. The cloth lapels have an inset of silk of the same tone as the coat. Light trousers are worn.

For evening dress, a *swallow-tail coat* of much the same type as the

Fig. 111. Frock Coat 1868   Fig. 112.
H.R.H. the Prince of Wales 1870

modern dress coat was universally adopted in the sixties (see Fig. 113).

SLEEVES. The sleeves of all coats and jackets during this period were similar in width and shape to those now worn. During the seventies, a narrow piping of braid was sometimes seen on the collar and cuffs of the ordinary coat or jacket (see Fig. 109).

WAISTCOATS of the same material as the coat or suit were now largely worn, but coloured or fancy waistcoats had by no means gone out of fashion. A single-breasted waistcoat buttoning high in the neck was in general use (see Plate XVII, and various Figs.), but the double-breasted variety with fairly broad lapels was still fre-

Fig. 113. Evening Dress 1865   Fig. 114. Frock Coat 1873

quently seen (see Fig. 114). A gold watch-chain called an ALBERT now took the place of the gold neck-chain previously worn.

SHIRTS. A characteristic shirt of the period (Fig. 115) was made of spotted cotton material, made very full and gathered into the neckband. It was cut without a seam on the shoulders and buttoned down the front. The extremely full sleeve was gathered into the armhole (which came down well below the shoulder) and was again gathered into the wristband. Striped shirts of similar shape were also worn.

NECKWEAR. The 'choker' collar was largely superseded in the sixties by a turn-down collar worn with a small tie or loose neckcloth. Many

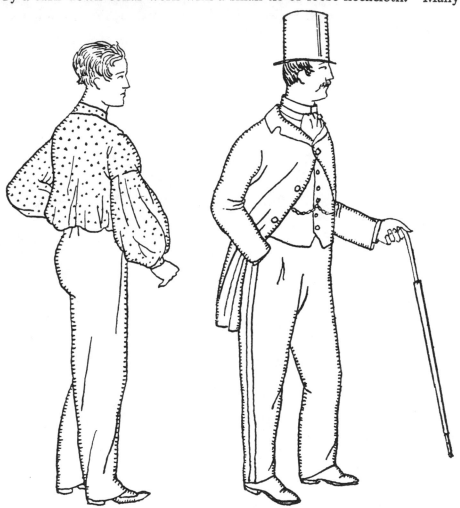

Fig. 115. Shirt of the 60's   Fig. 116. A Swell 1860

men, however, still affected the black stock and pointed collar until well on in the seventies. The narrow tie of the sixties, fastened in front in a small knot or bow, was popular with younger men (see Plate XVII), whilst older men preferred the neckcloth (see Fig. 110). A white tie fastened in a bow was *de rigueur* for evening wear (see Fig. 113). During the sixties a high round collar appeared (see Fig.

116), whilst a low turn-down collar, frequently striped, was popular in the seventies (see Figs. 109 and 117). *Tie-pins* were often worn.

OVERCOATS continued to be worn, of both the single- and double-

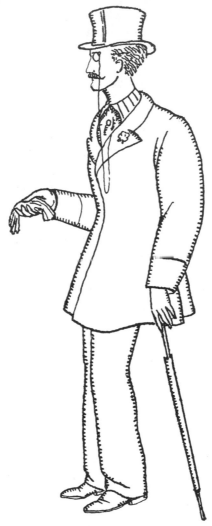

Fig. 117. A Smart Man of the 60's

breasted variety. The loose, single-breasted *Raglan* maintained its popularity (see Fig. 117).

CLOAKS AND CAPES. The cloak as now worn was shorter and closer-fitting than during the preceding period, and had a circular cape and two long openings through which the arms could be passed. This garment was sometimes called an INVERNESS or ULSTER. Cloaks for evening wear often had a small velvet collar in addition to the circular cape.

TROUSERS were long and fairly loose, and of course innocent of any turn-up at the bottom. They continued to be buttoned down the front and were generally made with side-pockets. In 1865, trousers were narrow at the top, wide at the knee, and fairly tight again below the knee.

Around the year 1866, tight-fitting trousers were much in favour among the more dashing young 'swells'. This was a vogue copied from the exquisites of the *beau monde* in Paris, whose outfit for evening wear comprised a cut-away dress coat, with rather full sleeves, dress waistcoat, pleated shirt, white tie, tight trousers, and highly polished square-toed boots. A very tall silk hat of chimney-pot shape, wide and flat in the brim, was worn, and the inevitable wax-pointed moustache and imperial *à l'Empereur*.

The English swell of 1866 is represented in Fig. 118 in the full glory of walking dress. He wears a black tail-coat, fastened with one button, over a low-cut light waistcoat, a stand-up collar, striped tie, and lavender or lemon-coloured kid gloves. His tight trousers are striped and his boots are black with light cloth uppers. The topper is of light grey felt. The accoutrement of this immaculate lady-killer is completed by the indispensable monocle, buttonhole, and walking-stick. It must have greatly distressed this young man and his coterie to learn of the tailors' strike, which occurred in 1867. During the whole of this period trousers were frequently made of the same material as the coat, although large plaids were also much in favour (see Plate XVII). Braid was sometimes worn down the sides of the trousers both in the sixties and seventies (see Figs. 109 and 116). It was during this period that KNICKERBOCKERS,[1] or loose breeches gathered in at the knee, were adopted for sports wear (see Plate XVIII).

Knee-breeches, in accordance with regulation, were worn at Court Drawing Rooms.

COURT DRESS. Regulations regarding court dress for gentlemen during the whole of Queen Victoria's reign were very precise.

The dress was modelled on the fashionable costume worn in the seventeen-seventies, except for the hairdressing, which continued throuhout the reigns of George III, of George IV, and William IV (see Fig. 119).

---

[1] Their name is said to have been given to them in 1859 from their resemblance to the knee-breeches of the Dutchmen in Cruikshank's illustrations to W. Irving's *History of New York*.

These regulations are as follows:

Coat: Black silk velvet, stand-up collar, single-breasted (for diagram see Fig. 3), seven cut-steel buttons on right front and seven notched

Fig. 118. A Masher 1866   Fig. 119. Orthodox Court Dress

holes on the left. The fronts meet edge to edge at a point on the breast, where they are secured with a hook and eye. Plain round gauntlet cuffs, with three notched holes and cut-steel buttons. Pointed flaps on waist seam, with three buttons, one under each point. Six buttons behind, that is, two at the waist, two at the centre, and two at the bottom of the skirts. Body of the coat lined with white silk and the skirts with black. Pockets in the breast and in the tails. Black silk 'wig bag', or 'FLASH', is attached to the coat at the back of the neck, hanging over the collar. Waistcoat: White satin or black velvet, no collar. Four buttons. Skirted fronts, pointed flaps to pockets, with three buttons under each flap. Breeches: Black silk velvet, with three small steel buttons and steel buckles at the knees. Hose, black silk. Shoes, black patent leather, with steel buckles. Hat: *Chapeau*

Fig. 120. Boy 1865

bras of black beaver or silk, cocked hat, with a steel loop on a black silk cockade or rosette. Cut-steel sword, black scabbard. White gloves, lace cravat and ruffles.

For correct wear at the Royal garden parties instituted in 1869 gentlemen's civil dress was regulated to top hats, evening coats, and morning trousers. 'Perhaps an attempt to accentuate the hour as between morning and evening', a writer aptly remarks.

Men's clothes at this period did not escape criticism, and the 'Illustrated London News' of July 1871, describing a Royal Garden Party at Buckingham Palace, wrote that 'the gentlemen all wore the most tasteless and unbecoming fashionable morning costume, the blue tail-coat (not a frock coat, which would do very well) with gilt buttons on it, the grey trousers, white waistcoat, and black cravat, in which no man should appear but on the stage of a theatre when a farce is being acted'.

Probably the following description of the clothes worn by Benjamin Disraeli, who in 1876 was created Earl of Beaconsfield, were also open to criticism. In middle life, while in residence at Hughenden Manor, a house purchased by his father in 1848, he was often seen 'in a brown velveteen shooting-coat with a flapping waistcoat, with long brown

Fig. 121. Boy 1862   Fig. 122. Boy 1877

leather gaiters drawn over his black trousers, a black "BILLYCOCK" hat, and a blue bird's-eye silk handkerchief tied loosely round his neck'. As he grew old he became very careless about his dress, and Ralph Nevill says of him: 'He wore, I remember, the most shocking overcoat possible, and was altogether very shabbily dressed'. The Earl of Beaconsfield and Viscount Hughenden died 19th April 1881.

BOYS' CLOTHES. Young boys at this period wore a jacket and waist-coat, both buttoning high up to the neck (see Figs. 120 and 121), or a sailor blouse (see Fig. 122). In each case knickerbockers were worn, and generally a round hat and horizontally striped stockings completed the outfit.

FOOTWEAR. The fairly heavy *lace-up boot* which came in during the fifties became more general, although *short Wellington boots* were still sometimes worn beneath the trousers. During the sixties, the lace-up boot attained a more elegant shape, and boots buttoning at the side were also fashionable (see Fig. 111). *Shoes* were seldom worn outdoors, except a light variety for tennis and croquet (see Fig. 164, Chapter VI).

HEADGEAR. The *top-hat* persisted in two forms, the straight *chimney-pot or stove-pipe shape* with an almost flat brim (see Plate XVII, and Fig. 116), and a curved shape with rather a large curling brim (see Figs. 111 and 117). In 1874, a grey top-hat was fashionable at the races. For evening wear the 'GIBUS', or *crush-hat,* was fashionable (see Fig. 113). A short, flat, felt hat with a straight brim was sometimes worn during the sixties (see Fig. 110), and the BOWLER HAT, or *Derby,* was well established by 1870 (see Fig. 109). *Caps* with ear-flaps were used for travelling, and a *deer-stalking cap* in plaid or tweed was in vogue for sports wear (see Plate XVIII). Cloth caps with a peak but without ear-flaps were popular among errand-boys, curmudgeons, and such-like low fellows during the sixties.

HAIRDRESSING. The hair was generally parted in the centre from front to back, worn rather long and waved, but flattened on the forehead. Side-whiskers became longer during the sixties, until the 'DUNDREARY WHISKERS' worn with a moustache gave the male countenance a surprising likeness to a Yorkshire terrier (see Figs. 111 and 113). MUTTON-CHOP WHISKERS were also worn, and the full beard was another modish decoration (see Plate XVIII). There was considerable scope for personal taste in the matter of facial adornment during the seventies, as it was equally permissible to wear whiskers only, or a moustache only, or whiskers and moustache, or beard and moustache.

SMOKING. The smoking habit still prevailed. The upper classes indulged in the cigar and cigarette; the lower (sometimes the upper also!) in the plebeian pipe. At Court the habit of smoking was not only disapproved of but prohibited. The Queen had a great dislike to tobacco, consequently all the gentlemen of her entourage, including even the Prince of Wales, had to forgo this solace. 'Punch' of 1863 makes humorous suggestions to those honoured by an invitation to Windsor.

In the middle sixties young coquettes smoked cigarettes when Mamma was absent.

WOMEN'S COSTUME

There was no Royal leader of feminine fashion in England after the Queen's retirement on the death of the Prince Consort in 1861, until the marriage of the Prince of Wales to Princess Alexandra of Denmark in 1863. Princess Alexandra gained the love and esteem of the public from the beginning, and as time went on she influenced women's fashions in clothes and deportment to a very considerable extent. In France, the Empress Eugénie was the supreme arbiter of fashion until her flight to England in 1870.

The Franco-German War terminated in 1871; the Commune and Louis Adolphe Thiers' Presidency followed. When Marshal MacMahon became President of the French Republic, the Princesse Metternich and the Duchesse de Morny (previously ladies-in-waiting to the Empress) retained their social status in the French capital, and led the fashions supervised by the celebrated designer, M. Worth.

During the mid-Victorian period, the *bodice* varied considerably from time to time, being sometimes cut to a point at the waist, when it was termed the '*corsage à pointe*', and sometimes made with a round waist and finished with a waistband or sash. Sometimes the bodice buttoned right up to the neck, terminating in a narrow collar, and at other times it was made with a square or V-shaped opening, revealing a *chemisette* of lawn or muslin. In fact the only feature of the bodice which remained constant was the universally tight waist. Sleeves of both the tight-fitting and loose variety were worn, and there were several special forms of the latter, known as the '*bishop sleeve*', the '*mandarin sleeve*', and the '*pagoda sleeve*'. Blouse-like chemisettes were frequently worn under dresses of wool or silk. These chemisettes of batiste, lace, or muslin were called '*canezous*', and were kept in place by a waist-belt with buckle. The *berthe* in various forms was still very popular, and was sometimes worn with a low-necked evening corsage. *Bodices* and *jackets* with *basques* appeared during the sixties, and the *casaque*, or overdress, appeared from time to time during this period.

The full skirt worn over a *crinoline* was now firmly established and for many years maintained its vogue in various forms. The 'Illustrated London News' of 10th January 1857 contained an advertisement of whalebone skeleton skirts and crinoline skirts from 7s. 6d., so that the modish silhouette was apparently within reach of all classes. The dress of which the crinoline formed the substructure varied slightly from time to time in the number and disposition of the flounces, and was sometimes worn quite plain.   In 1857, dresses with *double* or *triple skirts* ('*robes à deux ou trois jupes*') were very fashionable.   Another variation of the same year was the '*quille*' (so-called from its skittle-like shape)—pieces of silk, satin, or any other material, disposed longitudinally on the skirt, five or six inches broad at the base and tapering up to a point at the waist.   In the late fifties there was a revival of the eighteenth-century style in cut, materials and trimming, and by 1860 dresses '*à la Pompadour*' or '*à la Watteau*' were quite the rage. The crinoline easily lent itself to the imitation of the eighteenth-century hooped dresses, a fact of which dress-designers were not slow to take advantage.   During the later sixties, *paniers* and *bouffants* on the skirt prepared the way for the introduction of the *bustle* in the seventies. Throughout the mid-Victorian period there were frequent echoes of the eighteenth century, and indeed changes in fashion were so numerous that it will be more convenient to tabulate descriptions of various dresses from contemporary fashion notes.

Attention is drawn to an 'elegant *morning dress*' of 1857 in 'jaconet muslin, the skirt extremely full, worn with a very long *casaque* (a sort of tunic or overdress) made to button the whole length if required.   The sleeves are long and wide from the elbow, falling nearly square, and may be worn open (from the elbow downwards) or buttoned to the wrist.   There are very full undersleeves of muslin with narrow wrist bands, and a collar of embroidered muslin is also worn'.

An outdoor dress of the same year was of dark lilac taffeta, the skirt having three flounces edged with embroidery in shades of violet silk.

The 'Illustrated London News' of 1857 notes that Paris fashions were approximate to those of Louis XV and Louis XVI.   The same journal describes a 'ball-dress of white tulle over a slip of white *glacé*, the skirt formed of three double jupes of tulle gathered up in festoons by chains of pearls, the corsage draped with a bouquet of white camellias in the centre, the sleeves, exceedingly short, of a single puff and frill with an agrafe of pearls on each shoulder'.

Another *ball dress* of white tarlatan had a skirt formed of 'five flounces edged with white silk fringe headed by a row of plaid velvet ribbon, and a corsage of the fashionable square trimmed with the same ribbon and fringe'.

A '*home costume*' of 1858 in grey poplin had a skirt '*à deux jupes*'.   On each side of the skirt was a '*quille*' of blue silk trimmed with black lace reaching to the bottom of the first skirt.   The second or upper skirt had six graduated bands of blue silk   The bodice was a plain high shape, buttoning up the front, the waist '*à pointe*', and had a *berthe* of blue silk trimmed with black lace and full *bishop sleeves* with deep pointed cuffs of blue silk.

In October 1858, the 'Illustrated London News' notes that as a result of the Royal visit to Balmoral, 'fancy *tartans* in silk or poplin are being worn for morning outdoor dress, and the rich colours of the clan tartans show very effectively in satin or velvet for dinner or evening costume'. An *evening costume* of white muslin is also described, 'the skirt having three flounces, and the low corsage being finished with a berthe of Maltese lace and sleeves trimmed with the same. A sash of tartan ribbon is fastened in front of the waist with a bow and long flowing ends, and bows of tartan ribbon ornament the shoulders'.

A '*seaside dress*' of 1859 in light grey cashmere or delaine had a skirt with only one flounce at the bottom, bordered by a narrow scarlet velvet band, and a plain low 'body' (or bodice) round at the waist with narrow scarlet band, worn with a *chemisette* and sleeves of fine nainsook. With this dress was a *casaque* of the same material made very long, and having *mandarin sleeves* lined with silk and trimmings of small buttons and bands of velvet.

A *ball dress* '*à la Pompadour*' of the same year had a skirt *à deux jupes*, the first skirt of thin tarlatan with two *bouillons* at the bottom, and the second skirt of blue *glacé* trimmed by a lace flounce and *bouillons* of tulle, and caught up on one side by a group of roses. A branch of roses crossed the plain low bodice from the right shoulder to the left side of the waist, and the bodice was further ornamented by a lace berthe and had *jockey sleeves* trimmed with lace.

The 'Illustrated London News' of 1859 states that flounces are still fashionable on *crinoline skirts*, but they are not carried above the knee. *Pagoda sleeves* are most worn. *Waistbands*, fastened in front or at the side, with long flowing ends are still fashionable.

It was in the year 1859 that the crinoline proper reached its largest circumference, and from this time onwards its original circular shape gradually assumed that of an oval; the front slightly protruding at foot level and with all the circular fullness at the back. It was said that the Empress Eugénie appeared this same year 'without a crinoline', but this is not quite the fact. The truth is that the Imperial cage arrangement was pushed much more behind in a manner best explained by referring to Fig. 127 (see page 156).

At the end of the fifties, assisted by the art of the great Worth, the Empress rose to even greater heights of magnificence in dress. Charles Frederick Worth, the son of a lawyer, was born 13 November 1825 at Bourne, Lincolnshire — an Englishman! For seven years he was employed at a draper's in London. In 1846 he went to Paris and worked at the Maison Gagelin. Starting for himself at 7 Rue de la Paix in 1858, he founded the famous firm of dressmakers. His renown and indisputable taste brought him to the notice of the Empress Eugénie and from 1859 until the fall of the Second Empire in 1870 he created all her most important gowns and held the position of official Court couturier. M. Worth died in 1895 leaving two sons. Two grandsons carry on the reputation and traditions of this historic house, whose main purpose is 'to render women more beautiful, elegant, and smart'. Henceforth the Empress of the French, guided by this artist, appeared on various State occasions garbed in white—in dresses composed of multitudinous flounces of tulle, tarlatan, organdie, crape, gauze, etc.— excellent foils for her marvellous jewels.

On one occasion it is stated the Empress was arrayed in white satin with one hundred and three flounces on the skirt. At another State function she wore white tulle strewn with diamonds to the value of two millions. White gauze trimmed with silver and soft shades of mauves, pinks, and blues were her particular fancy, and most enchanting with her fair complexion and golden red hair! One has only to turn to a portrait by Winterhalter to realize the Empress *had* good taste.

This painter also produced at a later date a portrait of the Empress Elizabeth of Austria, wherein she is clad in a voluminous gown of white gauze powdered with silver stars. The Imperial coiffure is bedecked with stars of diamonds.

COURT DRESS. Court and official costumes of this period are well depicted in a picture, painted by C. Barrett and engraved by F. Stacpoole, which forms one of the Royal Collection. The subject is the last Drawing Room which the Prince Consort attended at St. James's Palace, in 1861.

Fig. 123 is an example of one of these Court costumes. The bodice and ample train were at this time usually of silk, satin, or velvet. The berthe of lace or gold embroidery was worn very low in the neck and off the shoulders, puffed sleeves of lace appeared underneath. Gold embroidery descended the open front of the skirt and surrounded the train. The underskirt was composed of rows of ruchings of gauze with lace flounces between. A diamond tiara and a cluster of Court plumes with a long veil constituted the headdress. Gloves were worn higher up the forearm. The *tout ensemble* had a distinctly Georgian character.

This style of Court dress was revived on the occasion of Her Majesty's first Drawing Room held since her widowhood, in 1868.

Later in this period the 'Lancet' had a word or two to say about low-necked dresses:

The 'Season' brings its grievance about low dresses.   What is wanted would seem to be a more elastic rule of the mode, enabling ladies to adopt on State occasions, as in private life, the costume which befits their personal peculiarities of figure and health.   In truth, 'dress' should be a matter of style rather than pattern. It is hopeless to expect any relaxation of the rule in favour of men who do not appear to the best advantage in tail coats, but that is no reason why women, who are perhaps too scraggy or weakly to appear in dresses cut low on the shoulder, should be compelled to assume an unsuitable or unsafe garb, with no

Fig. 123. Court Dress 1860

better reason than that 'it is the fashion of the Court'. Let the Court reform its fashion.

A *ball dress* of 1860 had a skirt with six flounces, a waistband fastened in front with a bow and long, flowing ends, a low corsage with a berthe,

Fig. 124. Ball Dress 1860

and a bouquet of flowers in the centre, and short puff sleeves with a small cluster of flowers on each (see Fig. 124).

Another *ball dress* of the same year had a skirt *à deux jupes* embroidered with posies, and a plain-shaped corsage with a narrow white edging round the top (see Plate XIX).

The 'Illustrated London News' of 1860 describes a '*dress for a young lady*', the *piqué* skirt having a white ground sprinkled over with small

Pompadour flowers, the *jupe* quite plain. With it is worn a *casaque* of light-coloured flannel, very long waisted, descending to a point and fastened with buttons. The sleeves, which are close-fitting at the top, gradually increase in width, and are drawn in at the wrist by an elastic bracelet. A plain linen collar completes the ensemble.

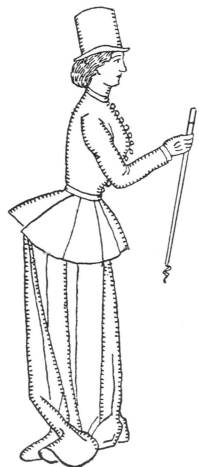

Fig. 125. Riding Habit 1861

An amusing comment on the vagaries of fashion in the early days of 1860 may be noted in 'Punch', where a writer objected to crinolines by reason of the 'well-founded fact that they are used for purposes of shop-lifting, and this has many times been proved at the bar of the police-court'.

The *riding habit* of 1861 (Fig. 125) is chiefly noteworthy for the basque on the jacket, and the characteristic shape of the top-hat.

An interesting 'seaside-dress' is described in the 'Illustrated London News' of 1861. It was a 'light fawn-coloured silk robe, the skirt bordered with a fluted flounce caught up on each side so as to resemble an apron; an open corsage, the lapels edged with fluted ruching, the waistband

Fig. 126. The Garibaldi Shirt 1861

fastened with a silver buckle; the sleeves wide and pointed and also edged with ruching; the chemisette and undersleeves in organdie muslin'.

An advertisement in the same journal (August 1861) points out the merits of the GARIBALDI SHIRT for ladies: 'In shape it resembles a gentleman's shirt, having pleats in front, turn-down collar and cuffs, and is long enough to put under the skirt of the dress, which is then finished with a band, or it may be worn *à la Zouave,* hanging over the skirt in front in "bag fashion", either way producing a graceful and elegant effect'.

Fig. 126 is a *morning dress* for December 1861.

The Garibaldi shirt—'an article that is now so much in favour—is made of very bright scarlet French merino, braided with black, and fastened down the front by black merino buttons. The shirt is made with a narrow collar, and straps on the shoulders ornamented with braid, and a narrow black silk cravat is worn underneath the collar. The sleeves are gathered into a wristband also braided, fastened by means of buttons and loops'. The skirt is of black silk, ornamented with a band of scarlet poplin at the bottom, the pockets being trimmed with the same material. The hat is made of black felt, bound with velvet, and is trimmed with red and white ostrich feathers. A net of the same red as the feathers is worn over the hair.

The shirt above mentioned was similar to those worn by the volunteers raised in July 1859 by Giuseppe Garibaldi (born 1807) in the cause of uniting Italy. In October 1860 this hero turned defeat into victory in a battle against the Bourbon Royalists on the Volturno. Shortly afterwards he met Victor Emmanuel II, King of Sardinia (1820–78), and saluted him 'King of Italy'. Garibaldi and his volunteers visited England in 1864 and were received with enthusiasm. He died in 1882.

Fig. 127 shows a *travelling outfit* for the year 1861. The dress and cloak are made of the same material—light-brown alpaca—and trimmed with dark-brown ribbon. A small green cravat is worn with this dress and a plain-stitched stand-up collar. A band of dark-brown ribbon is put on at the bottom of the skirt. The hat is of straw, having a black bow in front, with a black feather on the right side and a white one on the left falling from front to back.

In the early sixties lace trimming was lavishly employed, and a pink *glacé ball dress* of 1861 is described as having two black lace flounces on the skirt, and a silk *berthe* trimmed with two rows of black lace on the bodice.

An innovation of 1862 was the *trimming 'à la grecque'*, a form of key-pattern in ruched ribbon. Despite this classic echo the dress of this time was still full, the wide proportions of the skirt being principally confined to the lower portions. 'Training robes', we read, 'are not at all patronized by the *haut ton* for walking purposes, but only for indoor wear and dresses of ceremony'.

Fig. 128 is a drawing made from a portrait group of the Imperial family of France in everyday attire. The Empress's dress is simple

and composed of rich-coloured *moiré*, with braidings on the low
shoulders and at the cuffs.   The tight-fitting bodice fastens at the
front with buttons to match, and a narrow white collar surrounds
the throat.   The very ample skirt is worn over a fashionable crinoline,
which protrudes much more at the back than in front.

Fig. 127. Cloak-coat 1861

A record dating from early in 1862 states that the Empress of the French
had just adopted a new style of petticoat obviously to take the place of
the crinoline.   It is described as made of cambric muslin, six yards in
circumference at the widest point, and covered by nine flounces of still
greater circumference, the lowest of which was a mere frill; the second
a few inches longer and considerably wider, completely covered the
first; the third did the same to the second, and so on till one great flounce

fell completely over the other eight, each one of which, to arrive at the standard of Imperial elegance, was hem-stitched like a lady's pocket handkerchief, and the outer one in addition covered with embroidery done by the women of the Vosges. Somewhat expensive but no doubt effective!

A *ball dress* of 1862 in white tarlatan had a skirt *à deux jupes*, the first skirt nearly covered by narrow flounces of the same edged with lace, and the second skirt having a lace flounce headed by a ruche of rose-coloured silk. The low body *à pointe* (or bodice) had a lace *berthe* and short *bell sleeves* trimmed to correspond.

Fig. 128. The French Imperial Family 1862

A feature of the early sixties was the *Zouave jacket* for indoor wear (as distinct from the Zouave casaque for outdoor wear). This garment usually made in black taffeta ornamented with embroidery and braid, was shorter than the casaque and only reached about six inches below the waist. It was worn with a *chemisette* and full undersleeves of lawn or muslin. This form of jacket was equally popular for children (see Fig. 129).

A complete *costume for a girl of twelve* is shown in Fig. 130. The

Fig. 129. Little Girl 1860   Fig. 130. Girl 1862

jacket, somewhat reminiscent of a Spanish bolero, is worn over a full-sleeved chemisette of lawn. The full skirt in check material is ornamented at the waist by a wide ribbon bow with shaped ends, and is sufficiently short to display the plain untrimmed drawers. Light cloth boots with patent toe-caps and a small hat trimmed with an ostrich feather are worn.

On her marriage to the Prince of Wales in 1863, Princess Alexandra of Denmark wore a *bridal dress* of white satin over a full crinoline with numerous billowy flounces of Honiton lace. The flounces were headed by wreaths of orange blossom; and the beautiful lace veil was also surmounted by a wreath of the same. The Princess of Wales's going-away dress consisted of a fashionable gown of white velvet worn over the crinoline, a white satin bonnet with pale pink roses and an ample veil. A white lace shawl folded cornerwise fell from her shoulders. 'The footmen had gone before carrying the cloak, muff, cuff, and shoes, all ermine' (Letter from Mary Stanley 1862).

An *indoor costume* of 1863 in silver grey silk has 'a body (or bodice) opening *en demi-cœur* with lapels and collar trimmed with narrow cerise velvet and edged with a narrow fringe; the sleeve is trimmed up the back of the arm and has a deep *mousquetaire cuff*; the skirt very long and

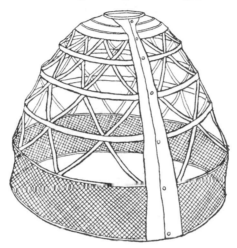

Fig. 131. The Crinoline 1863

full trimmed *en tablier* by six rows of cerise velvet, the trimming continued on the bottom of the skirt in a Vandyke pattern'.

In 1863, the '*robe courte*' (as opposed to the *robe à train*) was still fashionable for day wear, the skirt often being drawn up all round by interior laces to show a coloured *jupon* or *petticoat*. This fashion was evidently started in Paris in 1861 and copied from a freak of the Empress Eugénie which was recorded that year. Whilst staying at Fontainebleau, the Empress and her ladies played tricks with their skirts. They looped up their dresses over their bright-coloured striped petticoats in order that they might walk more conveniently through the forest glades.

As a general rule, the Empress was averse to launching a new fashion, and was frequently extremely *refractaire* in adopting innovations. She preferred her ladies-in-waiting to try out new styles before she would take to them herself. Worth, however, by the use of a good deal of diplomacy and persuasion, was able to mould her taste in clothes to a considerable extent.

In 1863 a special variety of crinoline was recommended to achieve the fullness of the skirt which fashion demanded. It was called the 'cage américain'.

Fig. 131 furnishes us with an example of the construction of the crinoline in 1863. It consists of five bands inserted with steel, attached at distances apart by criss-cross tapes. From the bottom band is hung a coarse network of horsehair about eight or nine inches in depth, also having a band of steel at its lower edge. This prevented the bottom part of the skirt from flopping inwards round the feet. The crinoline opens all the way up the front; it fastens by buttons or hooks fixed to a canvas panel.

The following statement from a magazine for April 1863 on the subject of the Crinoline is enlightening: 'Crinoline is not likely, as yet to be put aside, but it is modified; the steel petticoats are, like the skirts of dresses, in the shape of bells—very narrow at the top, and widening towards the bottom. This is much more graceful and becoming than the balloon-shaped crinolines of three or four years ago'.

A *seaside dress* of 1864 was of saffron-coloured taffeta, worn over an alpaca jupon vandyked and alternating with blue and white stripes. The long *vest* (or *jacket*) was provided with blue cuffs and lapels, completed by buttons and BRANDEBOURGS (braiding), and had a white waistcoat beneath.

A '*dress for a young lady*' of the same year was of white spotted foulard, the skirt trimmed with an ornamental ruching, and the *basque* and sleeves trimmed to correspond.

The 'Illustrated London News' of March, 1865, notes that 'for indoor wear the *Zouave vest* or *jacket* in cashmere or velvet is still in favour in Paris, and skirts are made in foulard or cashmere on purpose to be worn with these vests as well as with the braided *canezous*'. Pearl-grey crape or satin is reported as being popular for ball dresses, and 'the order of the day is simplicity united with good taste'. It may be noted that in spite of this 'simplicity' the crinoline skirt of 1865 involved the use of some ten yards of dress material.

The *Polonaise jacket* was revived in the sixties, and the 'Illustrated London News' of 1865 describes one of black velvet trimmed with fur. Another feature of the year was the *Señorita jacket*, without sleeves, usually made of coloured silk with a POSTILION (draped tabs) skirt at the back, all the edges of the jacket as well as the armholes being trimmed by a band of black velvet, and aiguillettes of black silk cord on the shoulders.

A *carriage dress* of 1865 in white foulard was ornamented throughout with violet silk trimmings and worn with a small *paletot* (or loose over-coat) trimmed with the same design.   Another dress of light blue striped taffeta had a jacket with aiguillettes (or shoulder knots) and a short tail behind.

An innovation of the year 1865 was a long trained skirt for street wear.   This was not, however, very generally adopted.

A *ball costume* of 1866 had a skirt *à deux jupes*, the first skirt of white silk ornamented near the bottom by a Greek border of narrow gold ribbon, and over this a tunic (bodice and skirt in one) made of green-and-white striped silk.   The skirt of the tunic was cut out in squares *à la grecque*, and edged all round by two broad gold ribbons.   It must not be imagined, however, that the temporary Grecian vogue did much to alter the extremely un-Grecian silhouette achieved by

Fig. 132 Afternoon Dress 1866

the universal wasp-waist and full skirt. In fact the gusseted skirt of 1866 required an even more capacious crinoline than that worn in the previous year, and this in spite of rumours that the crinoline was going out of fashion.

An *afternoon dress* of this year (Fig. 132) plainly evidences the amplitude of skirt still in vogue. This particular costume is of black taffeta with trimmings of indigo velvet ribbon edged with white lace. The collar and small epaulettes are also carried out in indigo ribbon with lace edging, and there is a ruched black taffeta flounce round the edge of the sides and back of the skirt.

At the opening of Parliament in February 1866, to the bitter disappointment of all, Queen Victoria, instead of wearing the orthodox Parliamentary robes of crimson velvet, gold, and ermine, was garbed in the deepest mourning, 'save for some slight badge and the Koh-i-noor on her forehead'. The 'slight badge' was probably the Star of the Garter; the gigantic diamond, which was set in her widow's cap, was presented to the Queen by the East India Company and recut in 1862. Fig. 133 is taken from a drawing of the Queen at this time, wearing indoor widow's weeds with the Ribbon of the Garter, and illustrates the foregoing description of her. The company awaiting Her Majesty's entrance into the House of Lords—the nobility of Great Britain—demonstrated by their gorgeous apparel their joy at beholding their sovereign once more.

Moncure D. Conway, in his 'Autobiography', says: 'I believe every gem, necklace, coronet, robe, and decoration belonging to the nobility was worn that day; the fullest Court dress, and the scene was billowy with necks and shoulders'. The following year Her Majesty opened Parliament again, and this time she wore black velvet and ermine, the insignia of the Order of the Garter, and a diadem upon her widow's cap and veil.

Queen Victoria was present at the wedding ceremonies of her three daughters.

At the marriage of Princess Alice in 1862 she wore woeful widow's weeds with much crape, but she graced the wedding ceremony of Princess Helena in 1866 by wearing semi-State dress. Her long train and voluminous skirt were of black *moiré antique*, of large watering, interwoven with silver. A white cap and veil, surmounted by a coronet of diamonds, and the Star and Ribbon of the Garter completed this very dignified costume. At this time Her Majesty displayed bare arms and magnificent bracelets, winged sleeves hung from the shoulders, open up the front and edged with miniver. Winterhalter painted her in a similar costume. The Queen appeared at the marriage of Princess Louise in 1871 dressed much in the same manner.

In May 1867 the foundation stone of the Royal Albert Hall was laid by Queen Victoria, clad in sombre black, a widow's bonnet, and

Fig. 133. Queen Victoria 1865

crape mantle. Surrounded by the crimson velvet and gold of Royalty 'her mind was in tune with her clothing'.

The Queen held the first Drawing Room of her widowhood in March 1868 at St. James's Palace, the official headquarters for all State functions. For some time past it was found that the limited size of the State apartments rendered them entirely inadequate to accommodate the increasing numbers of the company. Terrible inconveniences were experienced by the ladies attending these functions—a cartoon in 'Punch' satirizes these uncomfortable conditions. But the Queen would not deviate from prescribed rule. Any innovation on the procedure followed during the life of the late Prince Consort was distasteful to her. However, in the following year (1869) invitations were sent for a Drawing Room at Buckingham Palace, and not St. James's! In the July following, the first of the Royal garden parties took place in the grounds of Buckingham Palace. 'Breakfasts' they were then called, although they commenced at 4.30 p.m.

In 1867 the majority of 'walking dresses' were still made short, the 'robe à queue' (or 'à train') being reserved for evening wear. The 'robe à deux jupes' retained its popularity, and the upper jupe was often caught up each side as high as the waist, à la Camargo, to produce an eighteenth-century panier effect. Skirts were still enormously wide, but the gathers were pushed more to the back. The corsage was now frequently made with a basque behind, and jackets with basques were also worn. When these long bodices and tunics overlapping the skirt became fashionable, three or four intakes at the back and two intakes in the front at right and left were cut at the waistline to emphasize the figure at the hips. The materials most favoured at this period were velvet, drap de Lyons, poult de soie, and taffeta. For evening wear brocaded Lyons silks were much in vogue, a fashion patriotically inaugurated by the Empress of the French.

The year 1867 is noteworthy for another modification in the crinoline. The amount of materials required to cover this frame of necessity distended the figure in front. This fullness was now removed and the skirt gored to fit the figure at the waist, giving a more tapering effect. At the back the skirt was pleated or gathered as previously, the folds taking a more graceful contour over the crinoline from the waist to the ground. The skirt was still very wide at the hem. The original crinoline of entirely circular shape was no longer seen in the toilets of smart women.

The fashionable line of this year is seen in the ball gown, Fig. 134, composed of white satin ornamented with bands of narrow pale-green velvet ribbon. This is veiled with white gauze and draped with trails of pink roses and pale-green leaves. The same decoration is applied to the short-waisted bodice.

In the same year the Princesse Metternich is reported as having worn a 'tunic' dress at the races.

In 1867 the Princess of Wales suffered from a rheumatic affliction which threatened to contract her leg and make her a cripple. However, surgical skill triumphed, but for some time after her reappearance in public a year later she walked with a slight limp, aided by a stick. This limp was immediately imitated by some who are always ready to copy even the infirmities of distinguished people, and the '*Alexandra limp*' was adopted by various members of fashionable society!

Foremost among the revived modes of the eighteenth century was

Fig. 134. Evening Dress 1867

that known between 1865 and 1870 as the 'Dolly Varden', so named after the character in Charles Dickens's novel 'Barnaby Rudge' published in 1841. The story deals with the Gordon Riots of 1780 and the costume as worn by this young person (Fig. 135) is described by the novelist and is typical of the latter part of the eighteenth century. This style of dress consisted of a plain skirt, ankle deep, sometimes having a pleated flounce at the hem. Over it was worn a pointed bodice with a bunched and tucked up *polonaise* composed of some gaily flowered material over a BUSTLE.   A white frill or fichu surrounded the neck of the bodice and frills edged the sleeves.   A special item was the flat wide-brimmed Leghorn hat worn tilted forward and decorated with a few flowers.

Fig. 135. 'Dolly Varden'

A ribbon passing over the crown was tied behind with long ends under the chignon.

To quote a contemporary fashion-guide: 'Fashions have altered, times have changed, hooped petticoats have been in turn honoured and banished. . . .   Still, as an arrow shot in the air returns in time to earth, so surely does the hooped jupon return to power after a temporary estrangement from the world of gaiety'.

Fig. 136 shows the '*Zephyrina Jupon*' of 1868, a modified crinoline in the form of a metal frame with an open front. The contrivance gradually widens in circumference towards the feet, most of the fullness being at the back. It will be observed that this 'jupon' produces an entirely different contour to that achieved by the crinoline or cage of 1855 (compare with Fig. 106). The *crinoline underskirt* of 1868, (Fig. 137) is a similar modification of the crinoline petticoat of 1855 (compare with Fig. 104) made of tucked horsehair cloth reinforced with whalebone.

The effect of the '*Zephyrina Jupon*' is clearly shown in an illustration

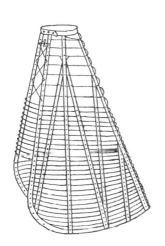
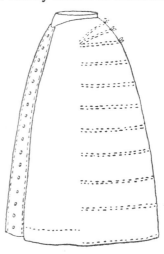

Fig. 136. The Zephyrina Jupon 1868   Fig. 137. Crinoline Underskirt 1868

of a *promenade dress* of 1868 (see Fig. 138). The costume is practically straight in front from the waist downwards, and widens out to the train at the back. The particular costume shown is elaborately trimmed with braid and bugles. The *jacket bodice* is moulded to the figure, buttons down the front and has a V-shaped opening at the side. The skirt is draped over an accordion-pleated underskirt, and ornamented with three artificial pockets in addition to the fringe of bugles. The sleeves are tight-fitting to the wrists, and have small epaulettes. A lace collar completes the ensemble.

The 'Illustrated London News' of 1868 describes a '*toilette de promenade*' of pseudo eighteenth-century style: 'the under jupe of pale-green taffeta ornamented at the bottom with three scallopped ruches; the *robe courte* (tunic or overdress) of foulard figured all over with small roses on a black ground; over the tight-fitting corsage is worn a *fichu Camargo*, the large lappets of which are tied in a bow at the waist'.

The same journal notes a plain white muslin with a *jupe à train*, and a high corsage with a '*fichu Marie Antoinette*' to which is attached a hood of rose-coloured taffeta, the whole being bordered with a vandyked edging of the same material.

Fig. 138. Walking Dress 1868

A *toilette* of 1868 in maroon cashmere had an underskirt trimmed with three little pinked flounces and an upper skirt trimmed with black lace, this second skirt being caught up behind under a *basque ceinture* with even pleats, an evident forecast of the bustle. The high body with black lace trimming at the shoulders had tight sleeves with mousquetaire cuffs of black lace.

An *evening dress* of the same year in rose-coloured taffeta had a *casaque Watteau* over the skirt looped up in festoons at the bottom by large ribbon bows.   The favourite dress *materials* at this time were taffeta, satin, and plush.

An innovation of 1868 was a sort of Spanish jacket called the '*Don*

Fig. 139. Walking Dress 1870

Carlos mantilla' trimmed with braid and fringe and having wide loose sleeves worn over lawn or muslin undersleeves.

In 1869, most of the dresses had a voluminous *bouffant* (or *puff*) at the back, the upper skirt being caught up at the sides with bows and forming a *tablier* (or *apron*) in front.

The 'Illustrated London News' of this year describes a '*dinner dress* of white Pekin taffeta with broad blue satin stripes; the skirt is pleated behind to form a natural *pouf* and trails a little on the ground; the low body is covered by a white barége *casaque* edged with a lace insertion upon a blue satin ground and a llama fringe; this casaque, which has long loose sleeves, is cut square upon the chest'.

Fig. 140. Walking Dress 1870

In 1870, the *bouffant dress* was much in vogue (see Fig. 139), but some gowns whilst retaining a considerable fullness were cut with a straight train from the waist (see Plate XX). For walking, the '*robe ronde*', without a train, was generally worn. Many of the dresses were still made in imitation of the eighteenth-century style with a *skirt à deux jupes*, the upper jupe forming *paniers* at the sides. The

Louis XV casaque was also fashionable. Violently shot silks and velvets trimmed with heavy fringe were much in use at this time, but some dresses of bright pure tone were also seen (Plate XX). Descriptions are given of a white muslin *pardessus* forming a round *tablier* in

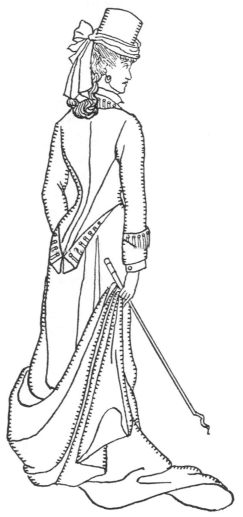

Fig. 141. Riding Habit 1870

front worn over a *robe ronde* in striped gold and white Pekin taffeta, and of a little *paletot* worn with a *robe à demi-train* of unbleached Indian tissue.

A '*toilette de promenade*' of 1870 is shown in Fig. 140. This is carried out in a striped material, sparsely ornamented with fringe.

The bodice is tight-fitting and the close sleeves have small epaulettes. The full skirt achieves a *bouffant* effect at the back and is further elaborated into a long wide train.

RIDING HABITS. Fig. 141 is a riding habit of the seventies carried out in blue, black, or green, cloth, and usually decorated with a little black silk braiding.

It is said that Napoleon III lost his Imperial crown through the misfit of his wife's riding habit. At a crucial moment during the disastrous August of 1870, the Empress was advised to ride in the Champs-Élysées with her ladies, but not being satisfied with the fit of any of the numerous riding habits brought for her inspection, she decided to abandon the undertaking. Had she not done so the Parisians would have been encouraged by the sight of their beautiful Empress and events might have been different. Both Empresses, Eugénie of France and Elizabeth of Austria, were excellent horsewomen and both had exquisite figures. The riding dress of the former empress was of dark blue cloth, its close-fitting bodice having a narrow basque, the seams and edge braided with black silk, and black silk buttons. The Empress Elizabeth's riding dress was also of dark blue cloth with gold buttons. Both ladies wore a high silk hat, with black or white gauze scarf, tilted forward over the hairdressing of the period as seen in Fig. 141.

The Empress of Austria frequently wore a small Tyrolese hat of pliable felt and finished with one little upstanding wing.

Throughout the sixties and seventies, a silk material called 'faille' was much in vogue.

In 1871 the *materials* most favoured were cashmere, rep, alpaca, and grenadine, all frequently trimmed with velvets of contrasting colours. For travelling, plaids in black and white or brown and white were in vogue, worn with a jupe of grey or black poplin. The *bouffant dress* was now *de rigueur*, and further ornamentations were added in the way of fringe, flounces, ruches, and bands of velvet. The *double skirt*, though less in vogue, was frequently seen. The addition of *basques* to the corsage was very prevalent. *Sleeves* were long, sometimes composed of four or five puffs and tight at the wrist, but more often hanging straight from the shoulder and widening to open at the wrist, revealing lace undersleeves. Another variation was the loose 'Pagoda sleeve', worn over a tight-fitting undersleeve of a contrasting material. The 'Dolly Varden polonaise', in chintz, cretonne, sateen, or velveteen, was still a popular feature.

The 'Illustrated London News' of 1871 notes that at a State Ball at

Buckingham Palace, the Princess of Wales wore a dress of pale green silk with *bouillons* of tulle, and a tunic of green silk ornamented with peacock plumage.

A grey poplin *walking costume* of 1872 had a skirt with two flounces just touching the ground, a *tunic with apron front* raised at the sides and edged with a flounce, a *jacket with basques* and sleeves open at the wrist, and a vest open at the throat with revers.

The 'Illustrated London News' of January 1872 notes that 'the *robe à la Louis Quinze*, with its general fanciful elegance and double jupe more *chiffoné* and *bouffant* than ever, still retains its place in the favour of Parisian *élégantes*. The under jupe is worn both long and full. Corsages are usually open, being cut square, *en châle*, or heart-shape. Sleeves are tight and trimmed with bias or slantwise bands of velvet or fur, and the open sabot shape terminating in a plaited flounce is much worn'.

The same journal describes a *ball dress* of white and green satin and Brussels lace. 'The under jupe of white satin is quite plain and forms a very long train. The upper skirt, made of green satin, is edged with deep lace, and forms a *tablier* in front and a *bouffant* behind, and has a demi-train caught up at the sides with branches of roses and falling in graceful folds over the white satin skirt. The low *corsage en cœur* (heart-shape) is bordered with lace and a full-blown rose is fastened on each shoulder.'

In February 1872 the 'Illustrated London News' reports that 'the favourite *toilette* for afternoon and evening receptions in Paris is the *robe princesse*, made of velvet edged with Chantilly lace, and open in front *en tablier* so as to display a skirt of satin or faille. The robe, which is tightened at the waist, falls behind in a long, square-cut train'. It is also noted that '*toilettes de promenade*' just touch the ground and at times are even worn with a demi-train.

The '*pagoda sleeve*' was still fashionable, as well as a *sleeve 'à la Louis Quinze*', the latter descending to the elbow with scalloped flounces veiled with a transparent flounce of Alençon lace.

Tunics à la Louis Quinze, Dubarry, or *Manon Lescaut*, in blue and *bouquetière* foulard were frequently worn over plain foulard jupons plaited half-way up. *Ball dresses* at this time had very long trains, puffs as voluminous as paniers, and very often lace basques falling over the latter.

A *walking dress* of 1873 had a skirt trimmed in front with a kilt-pleated flounce and at the back with flounces alternately pleated and frilled. With this was a double-breasted *polonaise* open at the throat and turned back with revers bound round with velvet. Quilted, kilted, and flounced silk or satin skirts were generally worn at this period.

Figs. 142, 143 and 149 illustrate the mid-Victorian idea of appropriate

Fig. 142. An Archer 1873   Fig. 143. Golf 1873

sports clothes for women. The former is a *costume for archery* (then a very popular pastime), with a close-fitting basque bodice, a full skirt trimmed with fur, with a *tablier* (or apron) in front and a pleated *bouffant* behind. The small round hat, akin to a man's bowler, is charmingly decorated with a large ostrich-feather. Gloves were worn for protection and were part of the equipment of both sexes. The *golfing outfit* (Fig. 143) is composed almost entirely of flounces. The bodice has a knotted lace tie over a frilled collar, and the rather

Fig. 144. Visiting Costume 1874

loose sleeves are finished with a wide frill midway between elbow and wrist. The lower part of the bodice forms a *tablier* finished with a wide flounce; the skirt has no less than three flounces, and is ornamented at the back with a *bouffant* bow and several wide ends. The hat, which has a forward tilt, is decorated with at least two ostrich-plumes and a flowing veil at the back.

A 'toilette de promenade' of 1874 had a skirt en train with a pleated flounce at the bottom and two rows of braid trimming above, and a tunic, or overskirt, made very bouffant and similarly trimmed with a pleated flounce and rows of braid. The jacket bodice had a basque

Fig. 145. H.R.H. the Princess of Wales 1875

at the back and sleeves widening to the wrist and finished with a narrow pleated flounce (see Fig. 144).

The outdoor costume of the Princess of Wales shown in Fig. 145 has a skirt à train with bouffant behind composed of black silk, the tablier (or apron) being edged with a wide tartan ribbon. The black velvet jacket is bordered with fur, and a stringless bonnet, veil, and muff complete this distinguished *toilette*.

An *evening dress* of 1875 had a skirt *en train* with five lace flounces headed by a double ruche, and a tunic, or overskirt, made very *bouffant*

Fig. 146. Evening Dress 1875

and similarly trimmed with a lace flounce and ruching. The bodice was cut with a square neck, edged with ruching, and the sleeves were trimmed with ruching and flounces (see Fig. 146).

The fashionable figure of 1876 was achieved by the use of a new contrivance called the 'TOURNURE'. 'This tournure (Fig. 147) will be found very effective in giving a graceful sit to the dress. It is made of black-and-white striped woollen material, and has a skirt buttoned to it. The skirt is trimmed with a puffing and two flounces of the same material.' This article is taken from a fashion book of 1876, and consists of a short underskirt to which the trained part could be buttoned. It is intended to be worn under the trained dress.

Another name for the tournure was the 'DRESS IMPROVER' (see Fig. 148). It is stated that this dress improver of 1876 'is made of strips of cane, closely woven, and being so netted it is capable of supporting any dress, however heavy, and being perfectly flexible, it resumes its shape

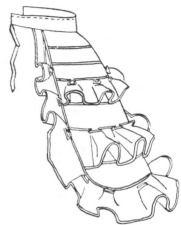

Fig. 147. The Tournure 1877   Fig. 148. Dress Improver of the 70's

the moment pressure is taken from it. This novel invention is tastefully covered with strips of French crinoline, and other suitable materials'.

The great designer, Worth, did much to influence fashion at this time. His favourite period of dress was the late seventeenth century and many costumes of the eighteen-seventies (for example Fig. 146, and Plate XXIV) recall the line of those in vogue during the reigns of William and Mary and Queen Anne.

An *evening dress* of 1876 in grey silk with skirt *en train* had an *overskirt en tablier* trimmed with two lace flounces caught up at either side with a large bow and made *bouffant* at the back with additional lace flounces. The bodice was cut cuirass shape with a lace chemisette and small puff sleeves (see Fig. 149). In this year the bustle became less pronounced, most dresses being fashioned to achieve a smooth effect over the hips, giving rise to a style which was sometimes rather loosely termed the '*princess robe*'.

The '*robe à la princesse*' of the year 1876 was cut without a seam at the waist and moulded to fit the figure from neck to hips. The skirt flowed in sweeping draperies caught low down in the centre of the back with a large bow or twist of velvet of silk, the remaining material forming a train like a peacock's tail.   To achieve this effect the train was lined throughout with stiff muslin and the pleatings which

Fig. 149. Ball Dress 1876

usually edged the train were underlaid with a lace-edged frill of muslin. Fig. 150 shows one of these 'robes à la princesse'.

Trains were worn out of doors as well as indoors.

A *promenade dress* of 1877 had a skirt *en demi-train* with deep pleating and a '*tablier*' (or *apron*) open at the sides and trimmed with a row of mother-of-pearl sequins.   The sides were pleated up and the back cut long.   With this was worn a *paletot bodice* open on each side over a lawn vest.   Pockets trimmed with sequins were placed on each side of the bodice and the coat sleeves were embellished with a deep pleating and double heading. A turn-down collar completed the ensemble.

A fashionable *walking dress* of 1877 (Fig. 151) is carried out in a

Fig. 150. Evening Dress 1876

plaid material, ornamented with black fringe. The bodice is cut the popular cuirass shape and finished at the neck with a plain linen collar. The sleeves are rather loose, and have ruffles at the wrist. The draped skirt is caught up at the side by a large satin bow, has three flounces in front and a moderately short train.

We have a record of Queen Victoria in semi-State dress in the portrait painted by Von Angeli in 1876.   In it Her Majesty wears a black satin dress having flounces of black lace laid on with narrow bias bands of black satin—a very usual trimming during the seventies.   The neck

Fig. 151. Walking Dress 1877

is cut square and not very *décolleté*.   The sleeves follow the line of those shown in Fig. 180 (Chapter VI), the shape being a special feature of Queen Victoria's sleeves.   Inside the neck and sleeves are frills of white muslin.   To the peaked widow's cap, similar to that described on page 191, is attached a long white veil.   The Star and Ribbon of the Garter and the Star of India, an Order of Knighthood instituted by Her Majesty in 1861, are worn.

When the Queen opened Parliament 8th February 1877, she wore a black velvet dress with a long train trimmed with bands of crape and edged with miniver. A long white tulle veil hung from her widow's cap of the same material which was surmounted by a small diamond crown.

Fig. 152. 'Zouave Casaque' 1860

'From the throne the eye turned to the scarlet-robed figure of him who was once plain Benjamin Disraeli, but who, carrying aloft the Sword of State, stood nearest the Queen—the Right Hon. Earl of Beaconsfield and Viscount Hughenden', so writes an eyewitness. It is noted that the Princess of Wales wore a dress of white brocade, richly embroidered in pearls over a jupe of satin to match.

In the following March the Queen held a Drawing Room at Buckingham

Palace.   Her Majesty, on this occasion, wore a dress and train of black satin, elaborately embroidered in black silk by some members of the Royal School of Art Needlework, which was under the presidency of

Fig. 153. Burnous à la Bédouin 1860

the Princess Christian of Schleswig-Holstein.   The Queen wore the usual cap and veil, surmounted by a diadem of diamonds, a necklace of uncut Oriental rubies set in diamonds, the Koh-i-noor as a brooch, and the Ribbon, Star, and Garter, of that Order.

Her Royal Highness Princess Beatrice was present and wore white silk, richly embroidered in floss silk, also by the School of Art Needle-work, and a train of striped velvet.

CLOAKS, COATS, AND MANTLES. These garments appear to have been as varied as the dresses of the period, and the lady of fashion was given

Fig. 154. Walking Dress 1860

ample choice of *pelisse, pelerine,* and *pardessus.* It will, however, be sufficient to indicate some of the more characteristic varieties. In 1857, dark *velvet cloaks* were chiefly worn, the favourite colours being brown, dark green, violet, and black, with trimmings of silk fringe and passementerie. For summer wear *Spanish lace mantillas* were much in vogue. Three characteristic features of the year 1860 were the

'*Zouave casaque*' (see Fig. 152), the '*Burnous à la Bédouin*' or Arab cloak (Fig. 153), and the '*Lodi cloak*'.   The latter was of velvet without any other trimming than a narrow ruching placed upon the interior edge, the sleeve in two pieces forming two points, a large tassel being attached to the lower one.

Fig. 154 shows a lady in *outdoor costume*.   The coat is one of very general design, fitting the waist and flaring out over the crinoline.   The sleeves are small at the armhole and wide at the wrist.   This coat could be carried out in a variety of materials with ornamentation of lace or fur.

The '*Illustrated London News*' of January 1862 has a description of a '*sortie de bal*' (or *evening cloak*) in white plush, ruched in at the back like a pelerine with a white satin bow and ends under the ruchings. The continued popularity of the *Algerian burnous* is noted, as also cloaks profusely ornamented with fur trimmings.   *Sealskin cloaks* were also much in favour.   The same journal in 1863 notes a *pardessus* in dark brown velvet trimmed with marten fur, whilst cloth *paletots* (or *loose overcoats*) were frequently worn.   In 1865 attention is drawn to a black silk *mantle* outlined with lace trimming, and *shawls* of black Spanish lace and Indian cashmere were always fashionable, *redingotes* and *polonaises* were further adjuncts to the walking dresses of the period, and in 1867 the same journal describes a '*pardessus Nabad*' of black velvet and a '*manteau Sultan*' of the same material. In 1869 mantles of black silk or velvet were much worn, sometimes trimmed with fringe and puffed out behind and at the sides and always ornamented by a large bow at the back.   Another variant was an embroidered *cloth jacket* fitting closely to the figure and trimmed with astrachan.   For November 1871 the '*Illustrated London News*' described a *mantle of redingote form* in black or brown velvet and a *casaque* of black cashmere trimmed with deep fringe.   The same journal in 1872 notes a garnet-coloured velvet *pardessus* edged with deep black lace and secured down the front with ornaments of passementerie and guipure, the garment being cut to form a small puff behind.   Striped *Albanian shawls* were a pleasing feature of this period.   Velvet pardessus and mantles persisted throughout the seventies.

MATERIALS. The names of some materials 'as now worn' at this period are interesting, and are as follows: Scottish cambric, printed *percale chinée*, Pekin Pompadour (figured with Chinese designs), *taffetas d'Italie*, grenadine, *barége* corded silk (a silk with a slight rib), *gros de Suez* (a silk which appeared in 1870 and was named after the Suez Canal), and foulard (a thin silk, usually printed in colours on a black or white ground).

English silks at this time were equal to those produced at Lyons and Genoa. Spitalfields, though but a shadow of its former self in the amount it produced, was as great as ever in massive richness and softness of texture and, for those days, excellent in colouring. In 1862 aniline dyes of various colours were introduced, and these superseded the vegetable dyes previously used. From about 1870 onwards, 'fanés', colours of a faded nature, were very fashionable. As time progressed, with the romantic enthusiasm for everything that was French, there was a growing passion for French silks. After 1865, the English silk trade declined especially as there was a great demand for fabrics of other kinds.

The 'Morning Post' for a certain day in November 1877 states:

We understand that a projected revolution in ladies' dresses, or at least in the material of which they are composed, is now agitating the town of Barrow-in-Furness. A local firm claims to have discovered the art of spining jute into a fabric combining the gloss and fineness of silk with the softness of wool, and singularly capable of taking the most delicate dyes. In order fittingly to introduce the new texture to Society a great Jute Ball is in preparation for a day in January next.

Reference has already been made to the sewing-machine in the preceding chapter (page 122). The inventor having died insolvent, this useful article, with the aid of the 'Morning Post', was brought before the notice of the public, and about 1860 many sewing-machines were manufactured. In ten years machines were in general use throughout the civilized world. 'The use of sewing-machines spreads more and more.' By the year 1877 the pedal sewing-machine had made its appearance.

UNDERCLOTHES continued to be more than adequate, except in the evenings, when a certain curtailment was necessary owing to the fashion of leaving the neck, arms, and shoulders bare. After the disappearance of the crinoline in 1867 ladies ceased to wear quite as many petticoats as formerly, but the cruelly whaleboned corset persisted throughout this period.

The corset (Fig. 135) is advertised in 1877 as 'thoroughly shaped and well-fitting. It is moulded by steam so that the fabric and bones are adapted with marvellous accuracy to every curve and undulation of the finest type of figure'.

When fashion decreed a short skirt for day wear, the colours of the upper 'jupe', or 'jupon' (as the petticoat was termed) became increasingly important. The short skirt also made it necessary to pay more attention to the stockings, which had for so long been invisible. In 1862 coloured stockings were much worn, but a fashion note indicated that the neatest were those marked with narrow horizontal black and white or other coloured stripes. A journal of 1863 describes the charming effect of violet stockings worn with a black poplin robe drawn up by interior laces over a coloured jupon with a cloth band. The 'Illustrated London News' of 1865 notes that white jupons are gradually returning into favour, but adds that 'another excellent mode when dresses are made to draw up is to wear a jupon of the same material; the effect is somewhat less striking certainly, but the object sought to be attained, the preservation of the robe, is thereby assured without that appearance of coquetry which is disagreeable to many ladies'. Another fashion note of the same year advises the choice of white stockings, except when coloured boots are worn, in which case the stockings should form a contrast as to colour. *Drawers*, reaching half-way down the leg, or even to the ankle, were still worn.

FOOTWEAR. Until 1860 there was little change in shape or material, and in the early sixties the heelless sandal was still in use for evening wear. From 1862 onwards heels were general on both boots and shoes, although high heels on shoes did not come in until the seventies. In the early part of this period both boots and shoes were somewhat plain, the long skirts giving little encouragement for the display of luxury in footwear. Boots rose about three inches above the ankle and were usually made of silk or cloth. They were either elastic-sided or buttoned at the side, and sometimes had patent-leather toes. When the short skirt for street wear became general, more attention was paid to the boot. The tops were trimmed with coloured silk, and laces of the same colour ribbon were employed. Chamois leather and bronze-coloured leather became fashionable in the sixties, although white or grey satin, kid, and coloured silk were still worn. A fashion note of 1863 mentions black kid boots with high red heels, and in 1864 lilac-coloured '*Russian boots*' are recommended for wear with a saffron-coloured dress. The 'Illustrated London News' of 1867 refers to high-heeled '*Arabian boots*' of scarlet or yellow leather, sewn and embroidered at the top with silk of some contrasting colour. In 1869 reference is made to Louis Quinze heels. Round toes came in with the seventies. In 1862 the new *French gaiters* for ladies and children were introduced.

HEADDRESSES. Bonnets of various forms were worn throughout this period, concurrently with a diversity of hats and toques. In the late fifties a rather small, tight-fitting bonnet was favoured (see Fig. 154). After 1860 the peak was again raised, and the space inside the brim where not occupied by the coiffure was trimmed with lace and flowers.

This type was known as the 'spoon bonnet' (see Figs. 155 and 156). A lace or ribbon flounce was added at the nape of the neck, forming what was termed the 'bavolet'. The bonnet was still secured by ribbons tied in a bow under the chin. During the fifties hats and bonnets were made of felt as well as of cloth and straw.

The 'Illustrated London News' of 1858 describes a bonnet of brown crinoline, having on one side a large rose, strings of brown ribbon, and a bavolet of brown silk trimmed with black lace. The under-trimming of the brim consisted of bouquets of roses. The same journal in

Fig. 155. Spoon Bonnet 1860

Fig. 156. Spoon Bonnet 1860

1859 notes that 'straw and Tuscan bonnets predominate, trimmed with cock or ostrich feathers or with a few large flowers of delicate shade, but that hats à la Diana Vernon with white cock feathers will still be fashionable for a sojourn in the country or for ladies en voyage'.

In 1859 the 'Spanish hat' was introduced (see Fig. 157), possibly a result of the increasing popularity of Biarritz as a seaside resort for English visitors. Another importation to England was the Scottish cap, shown in Fig. 158, which presented a somewhat curious appearance when worn with a chignon.

A three-cornered French hat with feathers set in the brim came in with the revival of the eighteenth-century style about 1860, as well as a small 'shepherdess hat', shaped like a plate or saucer, placed upright on the hair and rising high at the back. Other popular features of the sixties were the Spanish toque (see Fig. 153), a small bowler hat, and a very small 'pork-pie hat'.

The 'Illustrated London News' of August 1861 describes a Leghorn bonnet with yellow roses, black strings with yellow stripes, and a yellow bavolet, and also a Leghorn hat of flat shape trimmed with a large flat feather and a bouquet of roses.

Fig. 159 is a good example of the shape of *bonnet* worn at this time. It shows clearly how the curved front recedes to form the small back. To this is attached the '*bavolet*', or frill round the nape of the neck. Ribbon is employed to decorate this, and there is a large bow of the same in the centre. The '*brides*', or tie-ribbons, are exceptionally short.

Fig. 157.
Spanish Hat 1859

Fig. 158.
Scottish Cap 1859

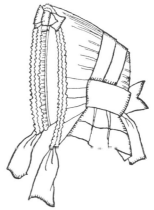

Fig. 159. The Bonnet of 1861

The 'Illustrated London News' of 1864 notes a *Louis Quinze Tuscan hat* decorated with eagle and ostrich feathers, and a bonnet of mauve crape, 'the quiet appearance of which is somewhat enlivened inside and outside by the addition of four white marguerites half buried in the crape'.

A fashion note of 1865 describes a white tulle '*chapeau Empire*', decorated with hedge-roses and rose-leaves and provided behind with a large bow and two wide bands of white tulle.

Figs. 160 and 161 are smart headgear for the year 1866. The former is a Leghorn hat, '*forme Japonaise*', trimmed with a garland of roses and leaves. The latter is a charming *fantaisie* called the '*Berger*', composed of a tiny circle of Leghorn, surrounded with a wreath of damask roses and tied on under the chignon with a crimson ribbon. Another hat of 1867 was of black tulle with clusters of white lilies of the valley arranged round the front.

In the late sixties the '*Metternich hat*' made its appearance. This was a small straw shape, tilted well forward on the front of the head and generally trimmed with flowers. A veil hanging from the back accompanied it (see Fig. 162).

The 'Illustrated London News' of 1868 mentions an *English straw hat* with a long veil of light crimson hanging from the back, a little black lace *toque* with maroon-coloured flowers, and a '*chapeau Louis XV*' of black lace, with black strings and rose-coloured flowers.

In 1870 the '*chapeau Watteau*' sustained the eighteenth-century note, and fashion generally favoured hats without strings, many being finished with a small veil falling behind. Another feature of the seventies was a small bonnet of a curved form (see Fig. 144).

Fig. 160.
'Chapeau Japonaise' 1866

Fig. 161. 'Berger' 1866

Fig. 162.
'Metternich' 1868

In 1872 hats were small and of a rounded shape, their turn-up fronts being reminiscent of visors. Mention is also made of a *round hat of Tyrolean form* trimmed with a large ostrich-feather falling down behind. The 'Illustrated London News' of this year also describes a '*beaver hat* with an ostrich-feather falling behind, whilst a duck's wing is coquettishly fastened on the left side'. The same journal notes an *Alsatian hat* with a little, round-shaped crown of black velvet, a lace scarf forming a bavolet, and black strings. A band of Chantilly lace is turned over the front, while at the top is a large Alsatian bow of faille ribbons with its four fringed ends falling down to the waist. Another novelty of this year was a *Charles IX toque* of black velvet, with a velvet aigrette at the left side and a large ostrich-feather falling behind.

In 1873 the feather-trimmed bonnet was still in vogue, and in 1876 small straw hats trimmed with lace and flowers of the '*Dolly Varden*' type were very fashionable. Throughout the seventies hats and bonnets were generally small, and worn well on the top of the head.

WIDOWS' CAPS. In the first years of her widowhood, Queen Victoria wore a widow's cap fitting close to the head at the back, with ruches round the top, all of fine white muslin. A long end with a loop, about three inches in width, hemmed an inch wide, fell on each side of the face. No collar or cuffs were worn.

In 1863 Queen Victoria's *widow's cap* was made on '*Marie Stuart*' lines without any tie-strings. A narrow white collar and cuffs were worn with a dress of black silk heavily trimmed with crape and jet, fashioned on the ugly lines of the period (see Fig. 133).

Despite these sombre clothes and her *petite* stature, Queen Victoria was *always* a dignified and stately lady. 'True Majesty was hers.' This was especially noticed by the Empress Elizabeth of Austria on the occasion of a meeting of these two great ladies. There is a portrait in the Hofburg at Vienna of the Empress-Queen Maria Theresa of Austria in her widow's weeds, seated at her writing-table. It is more than probable that the Queen-Empress Victoria had seen or knew of this portrait, and that it influenced her in the choice of her own widow's mourning. The personalities, conditions of life, and calling of these two Sovereigns were very similar.

HAIRDRESSING. During the late fifties, a fairly simple style of hairdressing was generally favoured, and this lasted until 1860. The hair was slightly waved, parted in the centre, and curved from the forehead over the ears, the back hair being arranged lower down on the nape of the neck (see Fig. 124, and Plate XIX). Sometimes the front hair was parted and plaited at the sides, the ends of the plaits being carried round and fastened at the back of the head by ribbon bows. The early sixties saw the introduction of the typical *chignon*, often enclosed in a net bag extending from the top of the head to the nape of the neck (see Figs. 152 and 153). In 1864 a round chignon was popular, with numerous curls hanging down at the back and on the shoulders. This coiffure was frequently embellished by garlands of flowers, lace, and ribbons, in keeping with the elaborate style of dress which prevailed. A fashion note of 1865 describes 'the latest style of coiffure for evening wear, the hair being rolled in front and curled behind, with an abundance of ringlets fastened by a golden comb'.

In 1866 the hair at the temples was slightly waved and also combed high, the back hair being treated less elaborately and either arranged in a roll reaching from ear to ear, or formed into a large bun enclosed in a net. Foundations were sometimes used. In 1867 mention is made of the '*coiffure à la Princess of Wales*'. For this style the front hair was waved and parted in the centre, the back hair being arranged in a massive roll terminating in long curls, with a single rose fixed over the right ear. An evening coiffure of 1868 was ornamented with wheatears and poppies, and in 1869 fashion decreed for evening wear a chignon embellished with a trail of wild flowers.

The '*doormat fringe*', immortalized by the Princess of Wales, originated about 1870. The front hair was curled, waved at the sides close to the head with a chignon behind. During the late sixties and the seventies, various elaborate coiffures were introduced, especially for evening wear. Some of these were of alleged historical design, such as the '*coiffures à la Maintenon* and *à la Sévigné*'. Hairdressing in the style of Mme de Sévigné, as it was interpreted in the seventies, is shown in Fig. 150. Other coiffures worn at this period were of mythological origin, such as the '*coiffure à la Ceres*'. Several features were common to all, the hair was combed away from the forehead, with the exception of a slight fringe, and the back hair was arranged in rolls which came down to the nape of the neck. '*Love-locks*' were pinned on as an additional embellishment. Other fashionable adornments were artificial flowers, including nasturtiums and even thistles. A characteristic coiffure of 1870 is seen in Plate XX. In a fashion journal of 1871, attention is drawn to the vogue for scarf-veils falling over the chignon, which in its turn falls down at the back of the neck. In 1872 the '*coiffure à la Louis XIV* and *Louis XV*' was popular, the hair being thrown up in front and hanging behind like a loose chignon in a thick net, usually made of chenille. Hair ornaments for the same year were generally composed of a tuft of flowers placed on the very summit of the head, with trails of foliage or ribbon falling down the back even to the waist. In the 'Illustrated London News' of 1873 was an advertisement of coils of long hair and *Spanish combs* with a curl falling on the neck. In 1874 the massive plaited roll still persisted (see Fig. 144), whilst in 1875 the raised roll on top of the head with floral decoration was very popular (Fig. 149). A coiffure of 1876 is shown in Fig. 149.

GLOVES were now considered of extreme importance, and were often beautifully embroidered on the back in the French style. For evening wear, a glove reaching half-way up the forearm was generally worn (see Fig. 149). Mittens had completely gone out of fashion. Broad BRACELETS were still worn with evening gowns, as were also bands of black velvet. NECKLACES of pearl or coral were highly favoured, with bracelets to match. Diamond jewellery was also fashionable, especially in the seventies. In the late fifties and in the sixties, as an alternative to the jewelled necklace, *collarettes* of black velvet were often worn, fastened in front with a pearl brooch, or carrying a large cameo or locket.   The tightly-packed BOUQUET was a charming addition to evening dress at the beginning of this period (see Plate XIX), and FANS were always *de rigueur*.   During the early sixties, little straw fans mixed with ribbon in a variety of colours were frequently seen.   HANDBAGS of silk or velvet decorated with beads, sequins or bullion were much in use.   PARASOLS were of various shapes and materials, chequered silk being especially favoured.   They were frequently ornamented with fringe, and the stick was generally longer than that used in the preceding period (see Fig. 139).   During the seventies parasols were of normal size.   The covering of the frame was elaborately decorated with embroideries, trimmings, lace, flowers, ribbons, and even tassels. The stick and handle were frequently carved, having bows of all shapes and sizes attached to them.   The very smartest parasols had much longer sticks than those previously in use and the handle was often placed at the reverse end so that the parasol was carried upside-down (see Fig. 144).

STAGE COSTUME. The most important theatrical management of this period was that of 'the Bancrofts' who continued the good work begun by Charles Kean.   Marie Wilton, born 1839, made her first appearance in 1856 at the Lyceum.   In 1867 she married Squire Bancroft, born 1841.   Their productions were noted for correct detail (or at least a conscientious attempt at correctness) with regard to scenery and costume. Mr. Bancroft was knighted in 1897.   Lady Bancroft died in 1921 and Sir Squire in 1926.

John Henry Brodribb, born 1838, known as the talented actor Henry Irving, was also a follower of the principles of Charles Kean.   His first success was in *The Bells* at the Lyceum in 1871, in which theatre he continued his management until July 1903.   He is recognized as the pioneer of the realistic school of acting.   For the stage costumes of this period one can refer to early photographs.   In opera there is Mme Adelina Patti (born 1843) as 'Juliet', taken in the late sixties.   Reference should be made to Figs. 132 and 134 for the outline of the costume.   It consisted of a white satin dress distended by the oval crinoline, open up the sides tabard fashion over an underskirt of satin—satin that stands alone, a short waist *à la mode*, ungainly sleeves with puffs up the back.   Her raven hair (she afterwards dyed it auburn to play Juliet) was most fashionably dressed with a chignon and long corkscrew ringlets hanging below her waist.

The Opera House, Cairo, was opened in 1871 with Verdi's opera *Aïda*.   This work had been commissioned by Ismail Pasha some time previously, but the date of its production was much delayed owing to the costumes and scenery, which had been made in Paris, being held up during the seige. Adelina Patti played the title role. Her appearance and costume in the part of the Ethiopian-Egyptian slave resembled that of a Red Indian! 'Nothing was lacking to complete the grandest

Fig. 163. Kate Terry 1866

entertainment ever seen!' This anachronism on the part of the fashionable *prima donna* is easily explained. Some Egyptian details were adapted to the modern (1871) style of dress with disastrous results. It is surprising that Patti did not wear, on this occasion, a modern ball gown — considered at this time quite admissible for costuming the heroine of any grand opera. Mme Patti married three times, two of her husbands being noblemen. She died in 1919.

On the frivolous side there was Kate Terry (1844–1924) as the hero in the burlesque of *Valentine and Orsine*.   Fig. 163 is a drawing made from a *carte de visite* photograph.

Actors, even in the Victorian era, to their credit, did make some attempt to reproduce the period of their characters in costume, although chin whiskers, or Dundrearys, sometimes appeared in classic or medieval plays.   Actresses, however, would persist in modernizing their appearance with many up to date touches—pomatumed hair, chignon, crinoline, bustle, etc.—as shown in many engravings and photographs of the period.

LIST OF ARTISTS WORKING DURING THIS PERIOD

Franz Xavier Winterhalter	1806–1873
George Richmond	1809–1896
Eugène Emmanuel Viollet-le-Duc	1814–1879
George Frederick Watts	1817–1904
William Powell Frith	1819–1909
George Scharf	1820–1895
John Tenniel	1820–1914
Frederick Leighton	1830–1896
George du Maurier	1834–1896
Heinrich von Angeli	1840–1925

CHAPTER VI

LATE VICTORIAN PERIOD (1877–1900)

CONTEMPORARY FOREIGN GOVERNMENTS

FRANCE: The Third Republic (1870 onwards)

GERMANY: William I (1871–88)
           Frederick III (March 1888—June 1888)
           William II (1888–1918)

AUSTRIA: Francis Joseph (1848–1916)

RUSSIA: Alexander II (1855–1881)
           Alexander III (1881–94)
           Nicholas II (1894–1917)

SPAIN: Alphonso XII (1874–86)
           Regency (1886–1902)
           Alphonso XIII (1886–1931)

ITALY: Victor Emmanuel II (1861–78)
           Humbert I (1878–1900)

INTRODUCTION

THE last phase of the Victorian era was, in England, one of unexampled prosperity and general well-being, especially during the ten years between the Jubilee of 1887 and that of 1897. General peace, and the enormous increase in trade and commerce, enabled the entire nation to enjoy a scale of comfort in everyday life such as had probably never been known before. With regard to the general tone of Society, the last twenty years of the century were considerably brighter than the two preceding decades. The venerable Queen partially came out of her long retirement, and the increasing influence of the Prince of Wales introducing a gayer note into the lives of the upper classes, social life became quite dazzling.

Naturally the period was not exempt from a few minor wars and rumours of war. In 1879 the Zulu War took place, in which the Prince Imperial lost his life fighting on the British side. In 1880 the Transvaal War broke out, but without very perceptibly shaking the foundations of Empire.

One of the foibles of polite society at this time was the fashion of 'lionizing' some personage of interest at the moment—an actor, musician, explorer, or what not. This habit (which had begun as early as 1862) became a positive craze in the eighties, and from it, aided by the growing art of photography, may be traced the development of press publicity as we now know it.

At this period week-ends were spent in Town, and the Sunday luncheon-party was a regular feature. Young men of fashion would engage a smart hansom-cab for the day, pay a round of visits in the afternoon, and then proceed to a dinner-party and a reception. It may be noted that the hansom-cab came into its hey-day in the eighties.[1]

During the whole of this period, Society willingly followed the lead of the Prince and Princess of Wales. The wit and affability of the former and the charm and elegance of the latter endeared them to every one with whom they came in contact. Although the Prince had a keen sense of humour, he was quick to resent any undue familiarity. At the same time unnecessary formality was distasteful to him. Both the Prince and Princess were in favour of leavening the strict German etiquette which had pervaded the Court ever since the marriage of Queen Victoria.

They not only received the aristocracy at their Royal residences but honoured the noble houses of the realm with their presence. They also widened their circle by including among their personal friends many eminent financiers, famous sporting men and women, wealthy commoners of note, and distinguished visitors from America. It was due to their Royal Highnesses's gracious reception of Americans that so many British peers selected their brides from among the beautiful heiresses of the United States.

In 1882 the Queen opened the Colonial and Indian Exhibition. From that time exhibitions of various types followed each other year by year. There was a note of tragedy in 1885, for that year witnessed the fall of Khartoum and the murder of General Charles Gordon.

In the middle eighties the public interest in Japanese art reached its culminating point. The more discriminating collected rare Japanese prints, embroideries, and other works of art, whilst the less discerning cultivated a fancy for Japanese odds and ends, such as sunshades, fans, and screens. In 1885 W. S. Gilbert's opera, *The Mikado*, was produced

---

[1] Mr. Aloysius Hansom, architect of the Birmingham Town Hall, built in 1833, invented in 1834 a two-wheeled carriage which took his name. Improvements on the original model were subsequently made by one or two eminent coachbuilders and the hansom-cab as it was known at the end of the nineteenth century was placed on the London streets in 1873.

at the Savoy, from which time no home was complete without its Japanese sunshade in the grate and its Japanese fans pinned on the walls. Whilst England was going mad over Japanese art, Japan was busily occupied in copying European dress and customs.

This led to a deplorable event in the history of costume. In 1886 the ladies of the Court of the Empress of Japan laid aside their picturesque and gorgeous robes for Western Court dress. The order is still rigorously in force, unfortunately, prescribing Western dress on all official occasions.

From 1886 onwards, Queen Victoria was seen much more in public, and in 1887 her Jubilee was celebrated with some State at Westminster Abbey. It is to be regretted that full Court dress was dispensed with, uniforms, and afternoon gowns for the ladies, being the order of the day. After 1887 the Royal Family became more and more occupied with public ceremonies of every description.

Dating from this time began a series of command theatrical performances, which were held in the Waterloo Chamber at Windsor Castle. Mr. and Mrs. Kendal and Mr. John Hare were among the first to be thus honoured.

The marriage of the Duke of York to Victoria Mary, daughter of Her Royal Highness Princess Mary of Cambridge and His Highness the Duke of Teck, was solemnized at St. James's Palace on 6th July 1893.

1897 was a year of exceptional social activity. The imposing pageantry of the Queen's progress to St. Paul's to celebrate the Diamond Jubilee took place in June. Throughout the Empire, her Jubilee was celebrated with tremendous enthusiasm. The British people had enjoyed a period of rest from war on a large scale since the Crimea and the Indian Mutiny, and this sense of peace and prosperity found fitting expression in the commemoration of Her Majesty's long reign of sixty years.

In 1898 the Sudanese War was fought, and Kitchener achieved the conquest of the Sudan. This was followed in 1899 by the disastrous Boer War, which did not reach a definite conclusion until after the beginning of the new century.

MEN'S COSTUME

There was a considerable amount of dandyism apparent in the dress of young men about town during the eighties. They conscientiously upheld the traditions of their forefathers that if one is somebody one must dress well. 'They felt they represented the aristocracy of England and must therefore keep up a well-turned-out appearance before the outside world.' [1]

The dandy of this period was known as a 'Masher' or 'Swell'. He adopted a certain languorousness and an affectation of speech of the 'haw-haw' type, a supercilious adjustment of his monocle, and strolled down Bond Street or rode in a hansom along Piccadilly clothed in a close-buttoned frock coat, slender trousers, patent-leather boots and SPATS, and a silk hat. Often this piece of head-gear was white with a deep black band. A buttonhole was a necessary adjunct.

As well as influencing manners and customs in the eighties and nineties, His Royal Highness the Prince of Wales, despite his figure (which even at the age of forty was very mature), set a certain standard of dress which affected not only his immediate circle but masculine attire in general. This Royal example, as usual, took some time to permeate to the lower classes.

The man about town in the nineties was as careful about his appearance as he was in the last decade. He was 'wont to pride himself upon the perfection of his tail-coat and the immaculate shininess of his top-hat'.[2]

During this period the complete *suit*, consisting of coat, waistcoat, and trousers, was almost universally adopted. The coat and waistcoat were usually of the same material, although coloured and fancy waistcoats were sometimes worn until the eighties. White waistcoats were again fashionable in the nineties. The trousers were also of the same material as the coat, except when a morning coat or frock coat was worn.

COATS were of several different varieties. The most usual was the ordinary single-breasted *coat*, or *jacket*, with narrow lapels, a rather small opening at the neck, and side-pockets. The coat was usually worn buttoned right up to the neck, or left undone except for the top button (see Fig. 164, and Plate XXI). A breast-pocket was sometimes placed on the left side of the coat. A *tail-coat* of the same material as the rest of the suit was sometimes worn even in the country (see Plate XXII). For more formal occasions the single-breasted *morning coat* was *de rigueur*, with a narrow collar and lapels, and rounded-off fronts to the skirt. The double-breasted *frock coat* was still fashionable, and for evening wear the *swallow-tail coat* was essential. An innovation of the eighties was the NORFOLK JACKET for sports wear (see Fig. 165). Coat-sleeves generally were similar in width and shape

---

[1] Ralph Nevill.   [2] 'Fancies, Fashions, and Fads', p. 193.

to those now worn. *Waistcoats* were almost always single-breasted and made to button high in the neck.

OVERCOATS of various styles were worn, sometimes double-breasted

Fig. 164. Croquet 1879　　　　　　Fig. 165. Shooting Outfit 1885

(see Fig. 166), and sometimes single-breasted. A loose, single-breasted overcoat of Raglan form was still popular (see Plate XXIII).

CLOAKS had gone completely out of fashion, with the exception of the *Inverness*, or *ulster*, and a cloak with a single cape for wear with evening dress.

NECKWEAR. The turn-down collar was still worn, but towards the end of this period it was much higher in form. A high, upstanding collar was also favoured (see Plate XXI), as well as a winged collar (see Plate XXII).   In the early nineties the stiff up-and-down collar was worn much higher and its corners became rounded.

A kind of *cravat*, or neckcloth, was much in favour (see Plate XXI),

Fig. 166. Overcoat 1885

as were also *knotted ties* (Plate XXII), and *bow-ties* (Plate XXIII). During this period the 'ASCOT' tie was introduced, which had much in common with the cross-over neckcloth of the forties.   It was generally made of black satin, with a jewelled scarf-pin inserted in the centre.

TROUSERS were made long and without a turn-up during the late seventies and the eighties (see Plate XXI, and Fig. 167).   During the nineties, trousers were sometimes worn turned up at the bottom. *Knickerbockers* were usual for sports and country wear (see Figs. 164 and 165, and Plate XXII). White breeches were the correct wear for tennis in the eighties (see Fig. 168). *Riding breeches* were popular,

Fig. 167. A Man about Town 1885

not only for riding (see Plate XXIII), being also worn by men aping their 'horsey' betters.

COURT DRESS for men remained the same as that worn in the preceding period (see Chapter V, page 142).

FOOTWEAR. *Boots* were habitually worn indoors and outdoors, except for certain special occasions (see Plate XXII). Both the lace-up and buttoned boot were in use. The *short Wellington boot* was still some-times worn beneath the trousers, and there were several varieties of *riding-boots* of semi-military form (see Fig. 166). Patent-leather boots

Fig. 168. Tennis 1885

were essential for smart wear, and often worn with light-coloured spats.

A light buttoned boot was worn with evening dress, except for balls, when '*dancing pumps*' or *court shoes* were necessary. Shoes were still very seldom worn outdoors, except *Plimsoll*[1] *shoes* for tennis and boating (see Fig. 168). *Slippers* were, of course, worn informally,

[1] Named after Samuel Plimsoll, M.P., 'The Sailor's Friend'.

and the woolwork variety flourished during this period. *Spats* were increasingly popular (see Fig. 165, and Plate XXIII).

HEADGEAR. The *top-hat* was still triumphantly ubiquitous (see Fig. 167), but the *bowler hat* was now increasingly popular (see Plate XXI, and Fig. 166). The '*gibus*', or *crush-hat*, was still in use for evening wear. The *straw hat*, or '*boater*', was another variation much in use during this period (see Fig. 164), and the *deer-stalking hat* was popular for sports wear (see Fig. 165). Caps were also worn for informal occasions and for sport (see Plates XXII and XXIII). Since the early sixties they had been a favourite head-covering with men and boys of the people, and towards the end of the century this type of cap, the sign of ascending democracy, was known as the 'vulgar cap'. It is to be regretted that even Oriental nations, renowned in the past for their beautiful and artistic apparel, have, on becoming westernized, adopted this inartistic form of headgear. A variety resembling a boy's school-cap was in use among adults during the eighties and early nineties (see Fig. 168).

HAIRDRESSING. The hair was now cut shorter, and a middle parting was generally favoured. *Side-whiskers* were still worn a good deal during the late seventies and eighties, but went out of fashion in the nineties. The *moustache*, with or without a beard, was popular, but quite a number of men were now clean-shaven.

SMOKING was now a commonly accepted habit, though still frowned upon by some. It was still necessary for the mere male to ask permission of the ladies before lighting even the comparatively harmless cigarette. The Prince of Wales was a great cigar-smoker, and in the early eighties he established the custom of smoking a cigarette or two after luncheon. Many smart Society women of the nineties surreptitiously indulged in the cult of 'my lady Nicotine'.

WOMEN'S COSTUME

The Princess of Wales' influence on feminine fashions was tremendous. She was always splendidly and tastefully costumed and the most graceful woman at Court. After the Jubilee of 1887, the Queen's age and infirmities not surprisingly precluded her from remaining the whole time to receive her guests at Drawing Rooms. It was her custom to retire before the end of the function, leaving the Princess of Wales in her place.

This was the period of the famous Society beauties, among whom

were Lily Langtry and Mrs. Cornwallis West and a little later the
Countess of Warwick, the Princess of Pless, Lady Randolph
Churchill, etc.

The photographs of these ladies and many others were in every
shop window, and it is said that people stood on chairs to see Mrs.
Langtry drive through the park.

Women of all classes studied their most minute changes of costume,
whether or not they had an opportunity of indulging in these vagaries
of fashion themselves.   In fact, Society beauties enjoyed at this time the
popularity which is now lavished on well-known actresses and film stars.

Young ladies of this period enjoyed more freedom than their mothers,
but still there was a considerable amount of time spent in the home.
Woolwork was still an occupation of the older generation.   For young
things, the vogue for elegant home accomplishments encouraged all
manner of arts and crafts such as macramé, linen embroidery of the
Swiss variety, lustre painting and flower painting on *terra cotta* pots
and plates.   Reference to any young ladies' magazine of the period
will enlighten the reader as to details.

In the latter part of the nineteenth century Lady de Grey, Marchioness
of Ripon, was the dominant social figure in London.   Towards the
end of the century there was a remarkable revival of interest in fancy
dress balls.   These picturesque functions were organized by the foremost hostesses of the nineties on an unprecedented scale of magnificence,
and were attended by all the aristocracy.   One of the most notable was
that given by the Countess of Warwick at Warwick Castle, 1st February
1895.   The costumes worn were those in vogue during the reigns
of Louis XV and XVI.   The Countess herself appeared as Marie
Antoinette in a dress of rose and gold with a sky-blue velvet train
powdered with gold *fleurs-de-lis*.   The 'period' was most excellently
reproduced and much credit is due to the beautiful Countess.   The
Princess of Pless represented Adrienne Lecouvreur (1692–1730) in the
part of some Greek heroine in an eighteenth-century stage costume.
A drawing of it is reproduced here (Fig. 169) because, not being so happy
in its correct eighteenth-century detail, it is a good example of how
modern (1895) touches could mar the *tout ensemble*.   The costume
was carried out in white satin and gold embroideries, the turn-up part
being lined with turquoise, and the jewels were turquoise and diamonds.

On 2nd July 1897—the Diamond Jubilee year—the Duchess of
Devonshire, known as the 'Double Duchess'[1] gave a magnificent
Fancy Dress Ball at Devonshire House.

[1] Her Grace was previously Duchess of Manchester.

All Royalty, except Queen Victoria, and everybody who was anybody were present.   It was said at the time that the most perfect representations were—the Prince of Wales as Grand Master of the Knights-Hospitallers of Malta (1570) in black and steel; and the Duchess of

Fig. 169. 'Adrienne Lecouvreur' 1895

Connaught as Anne of Austria.   The costumes were carried out in perfect detail and they both looked the part.   Cleopatra has always been a favourite character whose dress could be called 'clothes' and that's all.   Fig. 170 is a drawing of the costume worn on this occasion by Mrs. (afterwards Lady) Arthur Paget as Cleopatra.   It was designed and made by Worth.   The train was of black *crêpe de chine* embroidered with gold scarabæi and lined with cloth of gold. The skirt was black gauze and gold lotus flowers, down the centre of which hung a jewelled

Fig. 170 'Cleopatra' 1896

girdle. A striped sash, wide behind and caught towards the front, fell therefrom to the feet. 'The bodice, glittering with gold, and diamonds, was held up on the shoulders with straps of large emeralds and diamonds'. Both bodice and skirt followed the graceful lines of 1897 (compare with Fig. 196). The 'Egyptian' headdress was of gold, sapphires, emeralds, pearls, rubies, and diamonds—some faceted and some uncut—surmounted by 'the jewelled crown of Egypt'. Diamonds and jewels sparkled everywhere—real ones! The wearer's reputation demanded them.

During the whole of this period (1877–1900) the wasp-waist persisted, but the form of the *bodice* itself underwent several changes. In the late seventies and the early eighties, the so-called 'princess robe' necessitated a bodice tightly moulded to the figure, extending well below the waist and over the hips, and the '*cuirass bodice*' was very popular. A *basque bodice* was also favoured, sometimes achieving a military effect by an inset piece down the front known as the '*plastron*'. At the same time a shorter bodice terminating in a point a little below the normal waist-line was much worn (see Fig. 182).

In the late seventies an open neck was sometimes seen on afternoon gowns (see Plate XXIV), but in the eighties most dresses for day-wear were made with a high neck (see Figs. 181 and 183). An innovation of the eighties was the BLOUSE, thought to have been derived from the 'Garibaldi shirt' of the previous period. This was worn hanging over the top of the skirt all the way round and belted at the waist, producing a basque-like effect (see Fig. 171). During the nineties the bodice itself took on a blouse-like form and was worn with a pointed belt (see Fig. 195), but the corset-shaped bodice with a slight basque also found favour (see Fig. 172). *Sleeves,* up to 1890, tended to be tight-fitting and reaching nearly to the wrist, except for evening wear. During the late seventies, *mousquetaire cuffs* with a lace frill beneath were worn (see Plate XXIV), and *puff-sleeves* were another variation for evening gowns. In the nineties the '*leg-of-mutton*' *sleeve* made a startling reappearance (see Plate XXVI), but went out again with the beginning of the new century (see Plate XXVII).

During the late seventies, the *bustle* was well in evidence, achieved by much puffed and draped material (see Plate XXIV), though the popularity of the '*princess robe*' obviated any fullness in front or at the sides of the skirt. In 1880 the bustle was often dispensed with, although the majority of dresses were still looped up at the back. In 1882 the bustle was again received into favour, but only as a contrivance to support the overskirts which were worn above a tight '*sheath-skirt*'. By 1885, however, the bustle had reached a more exaggerated form than ever (see Fig. 181, and Plate XXV), although skirts without a bustle were occasionally in use for informal occasions (see Fig. 171). Even dresses for quite small children were made in ridiculous imitation of their elders (see Fig. 173). During the late eighties, trains were seldom worn except with evening gowns. In the nineties the bustle finally

Fig. 171. The Blouse 1889   Fig. 172. Evening Dress 1897

disappeared, and skirts though generally long and trailing were comparatively simple in cut (see Plate XXVI and Fig. 172).

An *evening toilette* of 1878 was described as a 'plain *princess robe* of *damassé* silk cut open at the throat and ornamented with a frill; elbow sleeves, *bouillonné* and edged with deep lace, a lace *Medici collar*, and a train of plain silk trimmed with a band of lace'. A green silk *afternoon frock* of the same year, with fringed trimmings and *bouffant* behind, is shown in Plate XXIV. The underskirt and front of the bodice are of a contrasting colour.

RIDING HABITS worn at this time differed but slightly from that shown in Fig. 141 (Chapter V).

The Empress Elizabeth, during her annual visits to England and Ireland, in the years 1878, 1879, 1880, and 1881, for the hunting season, was the admiration of every field. So closely did her well-cut habit cling to her lovely form that it was a common saying that she must have been sewn into it. Her jackets were of absolutely perfect build,

Fig. 173. Little Girl 1887

and fitted to her twenty-inch waist of exquisite and natural roundness. She never wore a flower in her buttonhole, or a neckbow, or a pocket-handkerchief protruding from the front of her lapel, as so many ladies did at this time, but Her Majesty carried a small black-and-yellow fan, not to shade her complexion, but to baffle itinerant photographers.

English ladies attempted to follow this perfection in the cut of their habits.

A characteristic *walking dress* of 1879 had a short round skirt of gathered silk, tunic, and *paniers* of figured percale, and a *basque bodice* of the same with a gathered silk '*plastron*'.

The æsthetic movement came into full flower in the late seventies and early eighties. This yearning for the beautiful—the 'too utterly utter'—which idealized idiotic poems, sickly colours, insipid flowers, languishing attitudes, and art drapery is caricatured by 'Punch'.   It is very happily exemplified in W. S. Gilbert's opera of *Patience*, produced in 1881.   Fig. 174 is a 'love-sick maiden', who glided through fashionable London life during this decade.   She wears an evening dress of

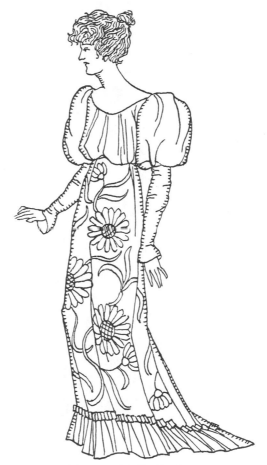

Fig. 174. 'A Love-sick Maiden'

faded green silk, the loose, rather clinging skirt being embroidered with yellow sunflowers and having a pleated flounce at the hem.   The blouse-like bodice has a fairly low neck, the sleeves being balloon-shaped above the elbow, and tight-fitting below to the wrist.   Neither corset nor bustle is worn.   The hairdressing is of the tousled variety popularized by the great Sarah Bernhardt.

A fashion note of 1880 describes an *evening toilette* in satin *glacé* which was cut in '*princess shape*' at the back, sides, and front, arranged as a petticoat and body, the skirt being entirely covered with draped white lace, an arrangement of lace being also made over the train. The body was composed of light-shaded silk, and had short *puff sleeves*.

An *outdoor dress* of 1880 is shown in Fig. 175.   The *cuirass bodice*

Fig. 175. Walking Dress 1880

buttons down the front, and has a fur collar and a lace *jabot*.   The tight sleeves are finished with fur at the wrist.   The skirt has a double flounce and trails on the ground at the back.   The small hat is decorated with a stuffed bird, probably a grebe.

Two fashionable *dress materials* of 1880 were Liberty velveteen and plush, or panne.   Liberty velveteen was a silk, short-pile velvet woven in cloth.   Plush was a long-napped material, like velvet but more glossy, manufactured from silk, cotton, wool, and any kind of hair.

In 1881 sweeping trains for street wear went out of fashion for a few years.

Fig. 176 shows the latest style of *promenade dress* for that year.   It

Fig. 176. Walking Dress 1881

will be noted that the general effect is one of slender elegance, the dress being moulded to the figure in one piece, with the exception of the pleated underskirt.   The only fullness of any importance is a slight bustle at the back.   The body part is seamed at the back to fit close to the figure.   In front, there is a slight fullness which is gauged round the neck, forms a series of folds at the bosom, and is gauged again at the waist-line, the remainder forming folds which are drawn

up to the side drapery. This side drapery is in turn drawn up to the
bustle behind. The underskirt is of striped material without a train,
and the same material is used for the pleated cuffs. There is a large
bow at the throat, and other bows are distributed on the upper skirt.

The 'new petticoat' of 1881 (Fig. 177) gives the side-view of the
general silhouette for that year. Sometimes, however, in order to
obtain a more tubular effect, the bottom frills at the back were dispensed
with. The petticoat was generally made of horsehair cloth.

A journal of 1882 has an elaborate description of a *ball costume* in

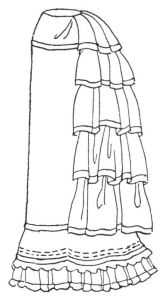

Fig. 177. The 'New Petticoat' 1881

rose satin and gauze. 'The satin train is trimmed round the bottom
with *bouillons* of gauze, relieved with flowers and foliage. The front of
the skirt is plain satin covered with gauze. The short tunic (or overskirt) is of gauze arranged in folds. The square corsage body has a
V-shaped *plastron* of gauze *bouillonné* trimmed with flowers, the arms
being sleeveless except for a narrow edging of lace on the shoulders.'

The appearance on the seashore of many fisher-girls with their skirts
caught up on their hips over their petticoats whilst unloading their
baskets suggested the 'FISHWIFE' *skirt* which came into vogue in 1882.
A portion of the front hem of the upper skirt was turned up, showing
the lining, and fastened close round the knees, the remainder hanging
in a loop behind. The dress itself was of plain material or, more
frequently, striped. The underskirt was usually close pleated.

Fig. 178 is a TENNIS COSTUME of 1883. It has a very tightly moulded bodice with innumerable buttons down the front, and tight sleeves which become rather full at the shoulder. The skirt has a series of pleats at the side, and there is a somewhat elaborately draped

Fig. 178. Tennis 1883

overskirt, complete with bustle. In fact, it is scarcely possible to imagine a costume less suited to sport of any kind. The little bonnet is secured with a bow under the chin and ornamented with the wing of a bird. High-heeled boots are worn.

In 1884 the bustle was again increasing in size, and there was a vogue for *kilted,* or *accordion-pleated, skirts* under paniers and a draped or *bouffant* arrangement at the back. An *outdoor costume* of that year

had a round skirt ornamented with a wide box-pleat in front and a
'*waterfall*' *back*, the sides being filled in with a zigzag of deep lace.
The high, pointed bodice cut in tabs had a *plastron* in front edged
with lace on each side, and three-quarter sleeves slightly full on the
shoulder.

Later in the same year long trains with outdoor dress reappeared in
Paris, and were, of course, immediately adopted by fashionable English

Fig. 179. Walking Dress 1884

ladies.   Fig. 179 is an *afternoon dress* of 1884 in which the overskirt carries out the 'waterfall' effect and continues on the ground for the

Fig. 180. Queen Victoria 1885

distance of a yard or a yard and a half.   This lady also wears a bustle of larger size.   The dress is composed of silk with flounces of black lace headed with folds of silk.   The tail of the bodice extends well

over the bustle, trimmed with a cascade of lace.   A *jabot* of lace descends
the full length of the bodice.

In 1884 the 'TAILOR-MADE' appeared.   Costumes for everyday
still retained their feminine characteristics of small waists, opulent busts
and large hips, but were often made of fine cloth, checked or otherwise,
with the masculine addition of velvet coat revers, cuffs, and suggestions
of mannish braidings and military frogging.[1]

The Queen-Empress was painted by Baron H. von Angeli in 1885 in
regal costume.   Fig. 180 is a drawing made from the portrait.   Queen
Victoria is robed in black satin relieved with white lace.   The bodice
is trimmed with lace at the neck and fastens with diamond buttons down
the front.   The open sleeves are edged with chenille over lace.   The
end of the train is bordered with a deep band of ermine.   Over the
lace veil is fixed the small Imperial crown of diamonds surrounded by
a row of pearls.   The Garter encircles her left arm (unseen), the Star
is on the left breast with the Ribbon and Lesser George over the left
shoulder.   The badges of the Imperial Order of the Crown of India
(instituted in 1861) and the Royal Victoria and Albert Order (founded
in 1862) are attached by their respective bows of ribbon on the left
shoulder.   Queen Victoria had a great partiality for Honiton lace and
most of her dresses were trimmed with it (see page 101).

An *indoor dress* of 1885 was carried out in black ottoman silk, trimmed
with black lace.   The train skirt was edged in front with a narrow
pleating, and covered with a *tablier* (or *apron*) of lace, draped in folds
and caught up at the sides with a large bow.   There was a large puff
at the back of the skirt, and the loose-fronted body had a vest cut
V-shape at the neck, and three-quarter sleeves with lace cuffs.   Another
afternoon frock had a petticoat or underskirt composed of a series of
restrained flounces, and a draped overskirt made very *bouffant* at the
back.   With this was worn a *basque bodice*, with buttons up the front,
a high neck with a narrow frilled edging and three-quarter sleeves with
plain cuffs (see Fig. 181).   An *evening dress* of 1885 is shown in Fig. 182.
An innovation of the same year was the so-called '*hussar jacket*' for
outdoor wear, made tight-fitting and trimmed with astrakhan.

The fashionable *tennis costume* of 1886 seems to have been somewhat
unsuitable for any sort of game.   It was made in plain or checked
French beige or cassimere cloth, with a tight bodice, a draped and
looped-up skirt and bustle.   A fashion journal of the same year describes

---

[1] As early as 1877 'Masculinity in Garmenture' was the subject of a letter dated April 1st
of that year, wherein some acidulous female protested against the masculine style of ladies'
dress 'in the present day.   At a little distance it is really difficult to distinguish a woman
from a man.   They wear men's hats, men's coats, men's collars, and men's ties'.

a *Goodwood dress* in checked canvas cloth with bustle, a front drapery of lace and a trimming of three ribbon bows on the left side of the bodice and the left side of the skirt. The same journal notes the popularity of the *sealskin jacket* with basque. The fashionable *dress materials* for this year were silks of various kinds (*gros grain*, ottoman and *faille*

Fig. 181. Indoor Dress 1885

française), plush, striped velvets, French cashmeres, printed delaines, checked zephyrs and velveteens.

The 'Illustrated London News' of 1887 has an advertisement of a *bustle* (price 2s. 6d.) so arranged with springs as to fold up when the wearer is sitting or lying down. Another kind of bustle made of braided wire was obtainable for the modest price of 1s. 6d. The same journal notes the popularity of the *Norfolk jacket* for ladies in black and coloured jersey cloth. A tussore silk *washable costume* of 1887 made in plain and check or stripe to match had a tight-fitting bodice with high neck, elbow sleeves with a small lace frill, and a looped-up skirt and bustle. A plaid *walking dress* of the same year with a tight-fitting bodice of a contrasting material is shown in Fig. 183.

Fig. 182. Evening Dress 1885

Many ladies attending the Drawing Room in 1868, the first held by Queen Victoria since her widowhood, adopted the French fashion of wearing their Court trains hung from the shoulders instead of the waist.

This Court train or *Manteau de Cour* had been introduced at the Court of the Empress Eugénie by M. Worth in 1855, and was a revival of that State garment worn by all ladies of the Court of the Empress

Joséphine (see Chapter I, Fig. 30).   It is obvious that this fashion was not followed at the Court of St. James's at so early a date as 1855, as proved by the picture of the last Drawing Room attended by the Prince Consort in 1861 and mentioned on page 150.

Fig. 183. Walking Dress 1887

This new Court train was made of every kind of rich heavy material, usually trimmed with gold embroidery or with other diversified ornamentation.   It was four yards long and one and a half yards wide at the base, tapering up to the shoulders.   Queen Marie Christine introduced this *Manteau de Cour* at the Court of Spain in 1879.   M. Worth designed and made the costume.

An example of the *dress worn at Court* during Jubilee year, 1887, is shown in Fig. 184. It is carried out in some delicate shade in rich satin. The corsage is plain, its only decoration being the deep lace which edges the low neck. The skirt with train is elaborately draped, with cascades of lace introduced. The Court train, hung from the shoulders, is of the dimensions given above, as regulated by the Lord Chamberlain's Office. Plumes are set upon the shoulders, and three more with a veil (in accordance with Court regulation) surmount the coiffure.

Court gowns at the Queen's Drawing Rooms were all made with a

Fig. 184. Court Dress 1887

tight corsage, practically sleeveless, and long gloves were worn reaching half-way between elbow and shoulder.

A fashion note of 1888 refers to 'an elegant *tea-gown* in black, or black and white, china silk with train and bustle, having an inserted

Fig. 185. Tennis 1888

lace panel to bodice and front of skirt, and sleeves nearly wrist-length finished with a lace flounce'.   There is also a description of an *evening costume* in Chantilly lace on a satin foundation with a jetted panel. This dress was completely sleeveless.

The *tennis costume* of 1888 (Fig. 185) contrasts very favourably with that of 1883 (see Fig. 178).   The blouse is not inordinately tight, and the skirt (although rather unnecessarily full at the back) would appear to give the player a fair amount of freedom. Plimsoll shoes and a somewhat masculine cap complete the outfit.

Plate XXV shows a *walking costume* of 1888. The black coat is seamed to fit closely to the figure, and has tight-fitting sleeves and a basque. The mauve overskirt has a long *tablier* or *apron* in front and a *bouffant* effect at the back over the large bustle. The underskirt of the same material is closely pleated with a small double ruching at the hem. The hat is of the flower-pot variety, adorned with sprays of flowers and a long veil which is brought round the neck in the form of a scarf.

The 'Lady' of 1889 describes an

evening dress of black and white strangely and very prettily blended. Half the corsage from the right shoulder to the left side is white and the other half black. On the white shoulder stands a high black butterfly bow and on the black shoulder a white one. The back of the skirt which touches the ground *en demi-train* is composed of folds of nun's veiling over which is thrown a veil of white spotted net. The front is of white silk trimmed with long bands of black and white ribbon placed diagonally, the white ribbon fringed with crystal drops and the black ribbon fringed with jet.

The 'Queen' of 1889 notes that 'dull and bright jet, rich tape guipure, and French lace ornament everything'. At a State Ball at Buckingham Palace in the same year it was observed that all the gowns were entirely sleeveless, and the corsage decorated with a bow or small bouquet on the shoulder. A smaller bustle was still universally worn, except with a few informal day-dresses, of the type shown in Fig. 171.

The 'Illustrated London News' of 1890 notes the vogue for *tailor-made costumes* in Scottish and Irish tweeds. Other *fashionable materials* were satins, mervs, and rich silk brocades, also a ribbed silk called '*bengaline*' and a soft satin known as '*surat*'. Bustles were still worn with evening frocks and garden-party dresses.

A popular garment for day wear was the JERSEY BODICE with black velvet sleeves and collar, the body of fine stockinet of any shade, with gimp ornaments round the shoulders and buttons all the way down the front. It is said that Mrs. Langtry first introduced the 'jersey' by wearing a blue-pleated skirt united to a tight-fitting bodice by a red sash.

A number of bodices at this time were finished with a *Medici collar*, and most bodices and jackets were made with '*gigot*' (or *leg-of-mutton*) *sleeves*. The vogue of '*tailor-mades*' still persisted, and Fig. 186 illustrates a dress of this style. The coat, waistcoat, and skirt are carried out in cloth. A panel with a floral design is let into the skirt, and a lace collar round the throat and lace cuffs are worn. Many of the tailor-made costumes at this time were heavily braided.

RIDING DRESS. The lady in Fig. 187 has not lost her riding-skirt. She wears a long-skirted coat over breeches and top-boots. This innovation of 1890 was not too popular, as the habit-skirt was considered much more elegant.

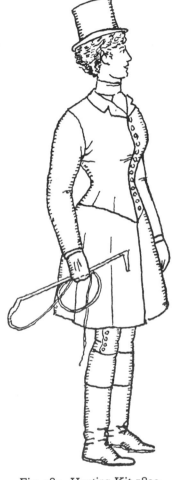

Fig. 186. Walking Dress 1890   Fig. 187. Hunting Kit 1890

In 1891 the bustle seems almost to have disappeared, but skirts were still worn full and long. The train made its reappearance in the nineties for both evening and outdoor gowns. Out of doors they were coquettishly uplifted, revealing quantities of rustling silk frilled petticoats *and* black silk stockings!!! (considered shocking).

BLOUSES were very popular throughout this decade, and the 'Illustrated

London News' contains a description of an *evening blouse* in coloured silk trimmed with chiffon embroidery, having elbow sleeves with a frill, a frilled collar, and a silk belt. Braided *jackets* were frequently worn.

Fig. 188. Walking Dress 1892

Gigot sleeves were universal, but a variation appeared in the form of a *gigot* sleeve rucked up the arm to form a series of puffs.

A YACHTING COSTUME of 1892 was composed of a full *bell-skirt* almost touching the ground, a blouse with turn-down collar and tie, and a jacket, open in front, with a wide turn-down collar and leg-of-mutton sleeves. A *walking dress* of the same year was cut in 'Princess style' to form a *corselet skirt*. Plaid skirts were sometimes worn, and a three-quarter length jacket with leg-of-mutton sleeves and fairly wide cuffs was very popular (Fig. 188).

The *wedding gowns* of Her Royal Highness the Duchess of York (now Queen Mary), worn on the day of her marriage in 1893, are to be seen in the London Museum.

A fashion-writer in the 'Illustrated London News' of 1893 describes a *gown* of stiff grey *moiré antique* made with huge sleeves to the elbow, and deep lace frills to the edges of the sleeves and as a berthe; also a silk *evening dress* covered with net embroidered all over with gold spangles, having sleeves of white silk muslin arranged in three full puffs to the elbow and then edged with a deep frill of spangled net 'so wide as to fall far below the arm when raised'. Another gown of pink-spotted silk had 'a very wide *bell-skirt*, eight or ten yards round the hem, trimmed round with three rows of silk ruching at the foot and a similar number above the knee'. The bell-shape skirt was now universal, and was sometimes gored to give the impression of being wider than it actually was. The addition of narrow little frills also gave the fashionable impression of width without adding perceptibly to the weight of the skirt. *Court gowns* were still made sleeveless, but had a wide, frilled collar round the shoulder in the form of a berthe. The sleeves on all other dresses grew fuller and fuller. For evening wear the sleeve was full and elbow-length, but for day wear it was full to the elbow and then tight to the wrist. *Blouses* were always popular, and *tea gowns* in black, white, or violet were considered extremely smart. The *Medici lace collar* was an additional ornament to a good many bodices.

The 'Illustrated London News' of 1894 notes 'an *evening dress* of white *crêpe de chine* with two bands of bright green crape carried round the bodice and a large rosette of same at the left side of the décolletage, the long green ends depending thence to the bottom of the skirt. The sleeves are immensely full puffs of white crape embroidered with silver spangles, and a flounce of silver embroidery finishes the train at the extreme back'. The same journal also refers to the universal *balloon-topped sleeves*.

The attractive *evening gown* (Fig. 189) of this year has a tunic suggestion of Irish lace over accordion-pleated soft cream silk. The double *balloon sleeves* and shoulder covering are of the same silk. Folds of blue velvet encircle the waist and sleeves, and a chic bow of the same decorates the tunic and another the hair-dressing.

In this year there was a good deal of discussion over the so-called 'rational dress', consisting of a rather full-skirted three-quarter length jacket or tunic and *knickerbockers* worn with gaiters. Needless to say, this great reform did not go very far, although some of the more adventurous women adopted knickerbockers for the new and fashionable pursuit of cycling.

Fig. 189. Evening Dress 1894

SPORTS DRESS. The energetic lady playing hockey in an ample skirt wears a belted blouse, the bottom part of which forms a frill below the waist-belt. The straw sailor-hat is held by a hatpin (Fig. 190).

Ladies took to bicycling about 1890. They then mounted the wheel wearing their ordinary skirts. When Society went crazy over bicycling round Battersea Park a special skirt was devised for them. Besides being convenient this new skirt was decidedly graceful.   It was shaped so that the back part followed the lines of the limbs over the seat, the side forming a sort of apron over the legs and hanging straight down on both sides.   Fig. 191 shows a CYCLING COSTUME as worn by the most enthusiastic cyclists, and consists of a bolero with balloon sleeves over a man's shirt with collar and tie complete; a short bell-

Fig. 190. Hockey 1894

skirt, black stockings, high, buttoned boots; a plate hat with Mercury wings and veil.

A *walking dress* of 1895 with plain skirt, three-quarter jacket, and balloon-topped sleeves is shown in Fig. 192. Attention is drawn to the masculine-looking collar and tie which complete the ensemble.

Fig. 193 is a Paris *walking costume* for February 1895, of cloth with a bolero, and band of coarse lace on the skirt. The balloon sleeves and godet skirt are becoming much more exaggerated. The toque is composed of puffed gauze and ribbon bows and ends. The repetition of the same ribbon in points and knot under the chin is a modish fancy.

A characteristic *evening dress* of 1895 is shown in Plate XXVI. The 'Illustrated London News' of the same year describes a *visiting dress* of white cashmere 'made princess shape, the bodice drawn over from the right shoulder to the left side of the waist and fixed there under a

Fig. 191. Cycling Costume 1894　　Fig. 192. Walking Dress 1895

big steel buckle. The skirt is plain but ornamented with three large steel buttons at the left side near the hem. The sleeves have quite a medieval look, being tight-fitting almost to the shoulder where there is a puff, and the high collar, pleated and studded with steel, carries out the *moyen âge* idea'. Another *ensemble for afternoon wear* consisted of a grey silk *bell-skirt* with an overhanging bodice of pink satin covered with white lace and having a deep collar and epaulettes of grey chiffon.   There is also a description of a smart *ball dress* of white silk with a flight of silver butterflies embroidered on the skirt and one huge butterfly forming the whole front of the bodice, which had big puffed sleeves.

Fig. 193. Parisian Gown 1895

A fashion-writer of 1895 commented on the craze for spangles on evening dresses, and also on the prevalence of *neck-trimming* in the form of a ruche or big black collar bow for indoor wear.   Attention was drawn to the ever-widening skirts, the absurdly wide sleeves demanding a corresponding balance of width below.   *Tailor-made dresses*, however, were usually made with plain straight-falling *tweed skirts*. The 'Illustrated London News' contains a reference to the 'sensible and useful fashion of wearing *coloured blouses* with dark skirts'.

In 1896 the enormous *balloon-topped sleeves* were still in vogue, also deep *corselet belts* sometimes with a short basque of lace round the back. The *Eton jacket* for ladies was very popular. Another innovation was the three-quarter length *tea jacket*, although the full-length *tea gown*, reaching from neck to toe, was still fashionable.

MATERIALS AND TRIMMINGS. Watered silks were much in evidence for dresses of all kinds, and *appliqué* lace and sequins were considerably in vogue as trimmings.

The bewitching BATHING DRESS shown in Fig. 136 is made of navy blue serge with trimmings of red and white braid. The skirt part of the tunic is slightly gathered in at the waist, or it could be cut all in one with the top part. Full knickers are worn underneath and the cap is of oiled silk.

The 'Illustrated London News' of 1896 describes 'a white satin *ball dress* with an *appliqué* of lace on the hem, the square-cut bodice and short very puffed sleeves being trimmed with bands of sable and white lace vandykes. Wreaths of roses are worn over each shoulder in lieu of shoulder-straps'. The same journal comments on an *evening dress of Empire tendency* with a high waist and train skirt carried out in faint green liberty satin. The décolletage was outlined with bands of green sequins and white pearl embroidery, the short very puffed sleeves being caught in the centre with a small band of the same trimming. A fashionable *walking dress* had a bell-skirt, balloon-topped sleeves and vest of rifle-green cloth, whilst the bodice was of black cloth trimmed with jet and finished with *epaulettes*. There was quite a vogue for all shades of green during the middle nineties.

Much comment, of not too flattering a nature, was made on the attire of the Queen of Great Britain when she paid her annual visits to the south of France 1889–97. It is opportune here to give a quotation from Clare Jerrold's *Widowhood of Queen Victoria* relative to this subject:

Like most of her country people of that day, she thought that any old clothes were good enough for travelling. . . . A broad-brimmed straw hat, a shawl and a black skirt which had seen much service, such as she wore in the grounds of Osborne or Windsor, are said to have become familiar in the towns of her holiday making, and were the subject of many jokes among our southern friends as well as in England.

A writer of a magazine article tells how 'once a new stableman at Windsor saw a little old woman examining the horses one day, and called out: "Hello! no one is allowed in here when the Queen is about!"'

upon which the straw hat, pointed shawl and black skirt turned round sharply, and the man's jaw dropped as he recognized the visitor'.

The 'Graphic' of 1897 (the year of the Diamond Jubilee), describes a *'costume for Henley* of white silken muslin with a thick muslin ruche edging the hem and tiny similar ruches on the seams. A frilled *fichu*

Fig. 194. Bathing Costume 1896

of canary muslin is draped over the shoulders, and a bunch of Maréchal Niel roses is tucked into the white silk belt'. *Fashionable materials* noted at Henley were white and cream muslins, both plain and spotted, delicately tinted organdie muslins, and white serge and alpaca. A *garden-party dress* of the same year was of rich emerald-green corded silk with a high collar and leg-of-mutton sleeves. Over the corsage was a *zouave* of fine cream net embroidered in small gold and silver beads and squarely-shaped at the neck both back and front. A fashionable *dress for the races* had a *bolero* of jet and steel embroidery over white satin. The usual *croquet costume* at this time consisted of a plain white *blouse* with *balloon-topped sleeves*, collar and tie, and a dark serge

Fig. 195. Walking Dress 1897

skirt and belt. Elaborately braided dresses were fashionable for day wear (see Fig. 195), and evening dresses were usually made with a long train and a square-cut bodice with balloon-topped sleeves (Fig. 172).

Full *evening dress* for the year 1897 is seen in Fig. 196. In this example the skirt and train are of rich substantial satin. Similar dresses were carried out in velvet or brocade. The pointed bodice is decorated with passementerie and folds of the material surround the décolletage and shoulders. The drapery forms an excellent background for displaying many magnificent jewels and orders. The characteristic coiffure includes the 'doormat fringe', a coil at the back, and a loop of

Fig. 196. Full Evening Dress 1897

hair known as the 'teapot handle'. There is a portrait of the Dowager Empress Marie Feodorovna of Russia, sister of the Princess of Wales, showing her dressed in a costume on exactly the same lines made in velvet and trimmed with sable.

A fashion journal of 1898 notes a *dinner dress* of pink satin with tiny chiffon frills, the corsage draped with a fichu of chiffon fastened by a large black velvet bow. The chemisette and transparent draped sleeves were of cream lace and a cluster of pink roses was rucked into the waistband. The 'Graphic' of the same year describes a *coat* and *skirt* in grey cloth, the collar, revers and *gauntlet cuffs* in white cloth with a narrow edging of sable. The three-quarter coat had gold buttons down the front and a white leather belt, and both coat and skirt were ornamented with braiding in gold and grey cord. The same periodical notes a *tea gown* of white *broché* silk with green satin stripes and pink rosebuds, having a wide *sailor collar* and revers of green velvet with *appliqué* of white lace and a border of mink. *Accordion-pleated skirts* were sometimes worn at this time, but skirts in general were frilled and flounced, often to the waist, but certainly round the bottom, and in addition were made to trail upon the ground. *Bodices with a yoke* were very popular, and the ubiquitous *blouse* was still frequently worn. Electric-blue was a new and fashionable colour during this year.

The 'Graphic' of 1899 notes a *dinner dress* of amber satin with a coat bodice of black jet on black net, a vest of white *mousseline de soie* and black velvet bows, and an underskirt of *mousseline* spangled with black jet.

In Fig. 197 is shown the fashionable sweep of the skirt and train of an *evening dress* of the year 1899. To achieve this the skirt is cut in three sections. The top part is moulded to the waist and hips; to this is seamed the second section cut on crescent-shaped lines. The third section or flounce is cut very much on the circle. The two seams are masked by a fancy trimming, and this trimming outlines the seams of the bodice. A circular-cut flounce passes over the shoulder, ending in a point in front at the waist, and finishes, or surrounds, the back of the low-cut bodice. Lace forms a kind of stomacher and also the underskirt. A black velvet band, known as a 'dog-collar', is worn round the neck. As an alternative, chiffon would be tied round, finishing in a large 'chou' on one side.

A SKATING COSTUME of the same year was carried out in mouse-grey cloth, and had a *zouave* of red velvet with bold embroidery in gold and coloured thread, the grey sleeves and skirt being similarly decorated. The *vest* of chinchilla was finished with fancy gilt buttons. A *walking dress*, described as 'very fashionable', had a *bolero* and skirt of caracal, the panel and lower part of the skirt being of black satin, as were also the vest, revers, and epaulettes. The sleeves were of a reduced leg-of-mutton form.

In 1900, the elaborately braided *walking costume* was still in evidence and skirts were generally made to trail upon the ground. The sleeves had only a moderate fullness at the shoulder, and the fashionable high neck, carefully boned to obtain the correct effect, was finished with a lace or other ornamental *jabot* (see Plate XXVII).   A smart *walking dress* of fancy foulard is described in the 'Graphic'.   The bodice was gracefully draped like a fichu and fastened by a rosette at the waist, the *sailor collar* in Liberty satin was trimmed with Venetian point

Fig. 197. Evening Dress 1899

insertion and edged with black velvet, and the same lace was arranged on the skirt above a deep-pleated flounce.   The same journal notes a *sable jacket*, with turn-up collar and cuffs of ermine and a lace jabot.

COURT DRESS. This débutante (Fig. 198), at one of the Drawing Rooms held in 1900, wears an elaborate evening-gown with train of lace or embroideries.   The regulation Court train is added to this gown, being attached to one or both shoulders.   The prescribed length was

four yards.   The width at the base was one and a quarter or one and
a half yards, tapering up to the shoulder.   These Court trains were
decorated in many and various ways and were sometimes lined with
contrasting colour and material.   The custom of carrying the Court
train over the left arm, when not in the Royal presence, dates from the
fifteenth century.   Three feathers and veil or lappets are set forth to
be worn by ladies on presentation in the regulations issued by the
Lord Chamberlain.

COATS, CLOAKS, and MANTLES.   In 1878 *cashmere cloaks* lined with
squirrel fur were very fashionable, as were also *mantles* and *jackets* in
Indian cashmere and Lyons silk, and *paletots* and *jackets* in diagonal,
checked, and fancy cloths.   Indian and China crape *shawls* were still
much in use.   All these were popular throughout the late seventies
and the early eighties.   An astrakhan trimmed coat for a little girl is
shown in Fig. 173.

The 'DOLMAN' was an outdoor mantle much in vogue during the
eighties.   Its chief features were that it fitted the curve of the back,
protruded over the bustle, had winged or cape-like sleeves open at the
sides, and fell in straight lines over the front of the dress—in fact the
pelerine of the eighteen-forties adapted to the line of the eighteen-
eighties.   The dolman was made of heavy material such as velvet, plush,
cloth, or fur, and trimmed with fringed chenille, lace, bugles, or fur.

In 1884 and 1885 *long close-fitting coats* of brocade, usually of a light-
coloured satin or silk ground with a large pattern in deep tones of velvet,
became the rage.   This fashion was inspired by the girl graduates in
the opera *Princess Ida* produced in 1884.   These coats were edged with
fur round the neck, and the wrists of the close-fitting sleeves.   At the
hem, which almost reached to the ground, was a band of fur as much
as twelve inches in depth.   With this coat was worn a round fur cap
with velvet crown having a quill at the left side.   A muff was frequently
carried.   Mrs. Langtry showed off this coat to great advantage.

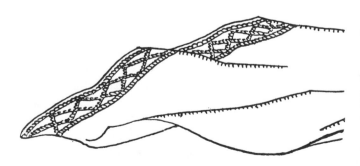

The 'Illustrated London News' of 1887 advertises a *manteau de visite* in beaded grenadine, handsomely trimmed with lace and jet fringe. In 1888 there was a vogue for *mantles* in black plush, *peau de soie*, and *moiré* silk. The 'Queen' of 1889 noted that long and short mantles were equally popular. In 1890 short plush mantles were general, as well as plaid *travelling cloaks* and *ulsters*. The 'Illustrated London News' of that year notes a three-quarter length *evening cloak* in sealskin shaped to the figure and having collar and cuffs of a contrasting fur. Reference is also made to a plaid *waterproof cloak* with cape. *Sealskin jackets*

Fig. 198. Court Dress 1900

were much in use as well as fur-trimmed *dolmans*. A characteristic garment of 1891 was a three-quarter length *cloak* in cloth with a high collar, cape-sleeves, and braid trimmings. In 1892 *black lace mantles* were popular for summer wear. A three-quarter length cloak, with cape-sleeves and an ornamental hood, and secured by cross-over bands in front, was worn in cold weather. The same journal for 1893 notes the popularity of capes, coats, and mantles, composed entirely of sealskin, or in a combination of furs. In fact, during this period, the *fur coat* really came into its own. The same journal in 1894 describes 'a handsome *black moiré mantle*, warmly lined, and fitting as tight as possible. The sleeves are very full and set into a rather deep cuff of white lace topped by a strip of ermine. A deep shoulder-cape of ermine is placed above small epaulettes of white lace, and the stole ends of the mantle are trimmed along their length with an ermine edging and band of lace'. Another mantle of black *moiré* was short and very full, topped with a deep falling collar of stiff white lace, with a Medici collar of chinchilla above the lace. There is also a reference to a long coat of moss-green velvet trimmed with bars of brown fur across the front breadths. The 'Illustrated London News' of 1895 notes that 'heavy *velvet coats* and *cloaks* are much worn' and describes a black velvet coat with a double cape collar of white satin embroidered lightly with jet and edged with a band of sable to each cape. This kind of garment was, naturally, unsuitable for really bad weather, when recourse was had to a sleeveless *waterproof coat* reaching to the ground, with a cape reaching below the waist, completely covering the shoulders and arms, and having two smaller capes superimposed over the shoulders. The same journal for 1896 describes a *pelisse* of purple-tinted cloth with velvet panel front from neck to toe, a trimming of jet and borders of chinchilla, and having balloon-topped sleeves made of velvet from wrist to elbow and cloth above.

Fig. 199 was described in 1896 as 'a suitable costume for a matron with a youthful figure'. The outstanding feature is the light summer *mantlet* worn over the fashionable bodice and skirt of the period. With the exception of the embroidered collar and revers it is entirely made of accordion-pleated frills.

A fur-lined *ulster* of the same year was lined with mink and had collar and cuffs of sable. A *travelling pelisse* reaching from neck to toe with balloon-topped sleeves was made in dark check with white lines running through it, and had a draped collar made of white cloth and fastening over at one side with a single button. The 'Graphic' of 1898 notes a 'waist-length *theatre cape* of white satin with revers of yellow velvet and ornamented with white lace *appliqué* and sprays of black jet.   A band of yellow velvet embroidered with black jet is carried round the cape which is edged with sable, and there is a frill of white lace and chiffon beneath.   The high collar is of the Medici style'.   A *fur cape*

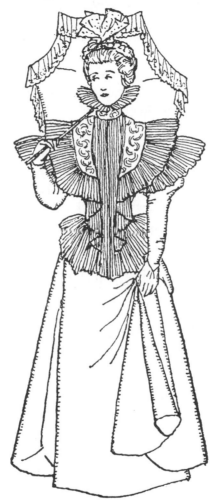

Fig. 199. Matron's Mantle 1896

for day wear was of sealskin bordered with chinchilla and had a grey satin bow at the back of the high collar.   The same journal in 1899 describes a *theatre cloak* of hyacinth-blue velvet with shaded chenille embroidery and border of chinchilla.   This garment had a stand-up collar and was very long, reaching fully to the ground.

UNDERCLOTHES remained much the same during the late seventies and the early eighties, but as the long reign of Victoria progressed, the need for a more delicate and fanciful style of *lingerie* made itself felt. The 'Illustrated London News' of 1892 has an advertisement of *nightdresses* and lingerie beautifully finished with French embroidery. The heavy petticoats of the early Victorian era had given way to expensive *silk petticoats* which were often elaborately frilled and flounced, especially during the nineties. *Openwork stockings* were now often worn, and there was a great vogue for black silk stockings even in conjunction with white or light-coloured dresses. White stockings were also worn and the 'Graphic' of 1897 advises the choice of white silk hose to complete the fashionable white ensemble for Henley. Stiffly wired or whaleboned *corsets* were universally worn throughout

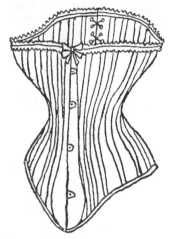

Fig. 200. The Corset of the 70's

this period (Fig. 200). The shape of the corset varied slightly, being longer in the waist towards the end of the century. The fashionable line of the moment can be seen in the numerous illustrations throughout the chapter. Even when the loose-fronted blouses of the nineties became general, they were always completed by a *belt* or *waistband*, thus ensuring the persistence of the fashionable wasp-waist.

FOOTWEAR. During the late seventies and the early eighties, boots were generally made of kid or other leather and secured by gussets of elastic web or buttoned up the side. During the eighties lace-up boots were frequently seen, and by the nineties practically all boots were fastened by buttons or laces. Leather boots were universal in the nineties, and throughout the whole of this period a high heel was in use, generally of the shape known as 'Louis Quinze'. Shoes were also high-heeled. With ball dresses and evening gowns, satin shoes or slippers were worn, usually ornamented by a ribbon bow or rosette. White shoes were worn during the nineties for special occasions, such as yachting and for Henley regatta. In the nineties a more pointed toe was in vogue both for boots and shoes.

HEADDRESSES. In 1878 bonnets were small and worn with or without strings. A smart bonnet referred to in one of the fashion papers was without strings, but trimmed with feathers and having a trail of ribbon down the back. There is also a description of a medium-sized velvet hat with turn-up brim all the way round and a drooping plume behind. For indoor wear *lace caps* with a ribbon were general, in shape rather like a small mob-cap. *Bowler hats* or *top-hats* were *de rigueur* in the hunting-field. In 1879, there was a considerable choice in the style of bonnet or hat. Two of the more popular modes were a small *bonnet* with a single ostrich-feather and a *beaver hat of cavalier form* with or without a plume worn at a rakish angle. Close *fur toques* were sometimes seen in winter, and both the bowler hat and low-crowned top-hat were in use for riding.

The 'Graphic' of 1880 notes the popularity of the so-called '*Gains-borough hat*', trimmed with three feathers of contrasting colours. In 1881 the same journal notes a small close-fitting bonnet of velvet and cream-coloured plush of the '*Mary Stuart*' *shape*, pointed on the forehead. For this style the hair was dressed in short frizzy curls to fill up the brim in front, and the bonnet was secured with wide plush strings tied under the chin in a large bow. The 'Revue de la Mode' of the same year describes a stylish *bonnet* of Leghorn trimmed with mimosa and roses of ruby silk, and having a maize-coloured satin bow and strings.

The 'Graphic' of 1882 states that 'the *matador shape* for hats is now in fashion and is very becoming'. Another popular mode was the '*Langtry bonnet*'. An example of this type was made of fine white or black twist straw sparingly trimmed with sage-green ribbon and a triple row of violets under the somewhat raised front. A becoming *Mary Stuart bonnet* was made of brown beaded straw and trimmed with brown beaded lace and yellow flowers.

In 1883 *bonnets* made of flowers were very fashionable, also pretty little white drawn satin bonnets dotted with pearls and with an aigrette in some bright colour. *Morning caps* were of muslin and raised mauresque lace with a band of velvet underneath the edge. The 'Graphic' notes a smart white plush hat trimmed with a coloured aigrette.

In 1884 velvet *toques* were much in favour, and there was a rage for red *bonnets* in straw, plush, velvet, or satin. A fashion journal of the year describes a bonnet of the new *'princess shape'* in brown fancy straw trimmed with brown velvet and beads and pale pink roses. Another pretty bonnet was of gold and Havant cord with a double diadem front, red and Havant velvet bows and a small wing. A characteristic bonnet of 1884 is shown in Fig. 179. A *'hussar hat'* for a little girl was made in blue velvet with a ruby satin bag hanging down the back.

The 'Graphic' of 1885 notes 'a hat of *Leonardo da Vinci shape* in cream flannel with a velvet band', also a 'pretty bonnet made of red currants'. *Hats* and *bonnets* at this time were as a rule very high in front, made of tulle spotted with gold, jet, or steel, and trimmed with fruit or flowers and fancy ribbon. Gold and silver trellis-work bonnets were popular. Coarse green *rush hats* were worn by young people in the country and these were trimmed with bulrushes, poppies or other field-flowers.

The 'Graphic' of 1886 notes that 'with the exception of a few small *capotes, hats* and *bonnets* are very high and fussy: sometimes all the trimming is on the top and at the back; flowers, feathers, birds, and ribbons; at others it is all in front with nothing but a small turned-up curtain'. During the winter of this year there was a revival of beaver for hats and bonnets.

Hats of the flower-pot variety with exceptionally tall tapering crowns and narrow brims, trimmed with bows of ribbon and flowers came into fashion in 1886. 'Punch' for 12th March 1887 caricatures one of these very tall head-pieces worn by the occupant of a hansom cab. When Marie Tempest took up the role of 'Dorothy'[1] in February 1887 she wore one of these hats in Act I. These hats were frequently known as 'steeple-hats' or 'three stories and a basement'.

A fashion writer in 1887 recommended 'for races and other outdoor sports, a Leghorn or other fancy straw hat or even a light cream felt', whilst *'bonnets* for dressy occasions are often mere puffings of tulle or diadems of roses'. The 'Graphic' of this year describes 'a quaint little bonnet of light steel-grey tulle in high puffs with a tuft of dandelions and their feathery seed-pods'. A very popular hat at this time was in the shape of an inverted flower-pot, but not so high as previously (see Fig. 183).

In 1888 the most popular form of headgear was a small bonnet with strings tied in a bow under the chin and usually worn with a veil.

[1] The period of *Dorothy* was supposed to be the eighteenth century!

The *flower-pot hat* was still in favour, but generally with a more definite brim (see Plate XXV). For tennis a rather boyish *cap* was worn (see Fig. 185). In 1889 a rather large-brimmed hat was frequently seen, turned-up at the back and having a cluster of ribbon bows on the crown (see Fig. 171).

In 1890 the fashion was for small *bonnets*, generally without strings, and worn with a half-veil reaching from the forehead to just below the nose. *Hats* also tended to be moderately small (see Fig. 186). The *top-hat* was *de rigueur* for hunting (see Fig. 187). During the year 1890 numbers of women wore a plain, hard straw hat, in shape like a man's '*boater*'. By 1892 this form of hat had become very popular, and *sailor-caps* for ladies were also in use. For more formal occasions, fashion favoured a hat with a wide flat brim in front, the brim being turned up at the back with a large bow placed thereon. One of the diminutive bonnets of 1892 is shown in Fig. 188.

In 1893 *bonnets* were worn fitting close to the head but trimmed on both sides. The favourite *trimming* was accordion-pleated lace, drawn together in the middle as though into a bow so as to spread up at either side. Detached bunches of flowers were also popular. *Hats were* large in circumference and worn rather at the back of the head. The 'Illustrated London News' notes a black chip-hat trimmed with three clusters of flowers, and a Tuscan straw trimmed with black feathers and satin ribbon. Spotted veils were fashionable.

A fashion writer of 1894 notes the 'vogue for flat *bonnets* of hoop shape or mere plates on the surface of the hair, with which only a little trimming is used, a bit of wired lace, a fur tail or two, or a jet comb with a scrap of ribbon at the back'. The '*boater*' was still in vogue, notably for sports wear (see Fig. 190). A hat specially recommended for cycling is shown in Fig. 191.

The 'Illustrated London News' of 1895 states that '*bonnets* are not made with distinct crowns (owing to the style of hairdressing) but flat, and only slightly bent round to follow the natural shape of the top of the cranium, coming well down to the ears so that they sit on comfortably'. The trimming at this time stood out wide on each side of the head, very often in the form of *Mercury wings* in horsehair-lace (or crinoline). Other favourite *trimmings* were spikes of flowers, frills of lace, jet ornaments, and net glittering with an incrustation of sequins or iridescent beads. The *toque* (or *stringless bonnet*) was very popular (see Fig. 193), also a *plate-shaped hat* worn on top of the head and trimmed with ribbon bows and ostrich or other feathers. The plain straw '*boater*' was still in use, also a *hat of tam-o'-shanter form* placed high on top of the hair. An unassuming boat-shaped hat of 1895 is shown in Fig. 192.

The characteristic *hat* of 1896 was a fairly flat shape with a small crown trimmed with ribbon rosettes and clusters of ostrich-feathers. A *toque* of the same year is shown in Fig. 199. White felt hats were much worn, and bunches of violets were very popular for trimming millinery. The 'Illustrated London News' remarks on 'the charming effect of a *tam-o'-shanter* jauntily set on one side of the head and decorated with a large bunch of white gardenias and a black and white osprey'. The flat *plate-shaped hat* persisted in 1897 (see Fig. 195), and the 'Graphic' of that year described a flat-shaped hat of black chip with high crown and clusters of black and white plumes.

In 1898 there was a tendency towards rather large *hats* worn flat or slightly on one side, trimmed with ostrich-feathers, ospreys, and large ribbon bows. Straw or tulle *toques* were also fashionable.

The 'Graphic' of 1899 notes the popularity of *fur toques* for winter wear, and also describes a toque of black and pink chenille and white tulle loops. The same journal in 1900 notes a *boat-shaped hat of Panama straw* trimmed with rosettes of white tulle and two quills. A characteristic large-brimmed straw hat, trimmed with ostrich-feathers and ribbon bows, is shown in Plate XXVII.

HAIRDRESSING. In 1878 the hair was generally parted in the centre and formed into coils high on top of the head, with further coils hanging down on the nape of the neck, and very often in addition a love-lock at the side. Sometimes, however, the hair was more simply dressed with a middle parting and a plaited coil brought low on the nape of the neck. Another variant was to have the hair thrown up in front, with a plaited coil, and hanging behind like a loose chignon (see Plate XXIV). A fashion-writer in the 'Graphic' of 1878 states that 'high foreheads are out of fashion, and if they exist should be hidden by a thick straight fringe or short frizzed curls'. The middle parting and fringe, with coils of hair on the nape of the neck, persisted throughout the late seventies and the early eighties. In the evening, the coiffure was often further ornamented by a floral wreath. In 1878, powder in various colours was used instead of hair dye. In 1882, the 'doormat fringe' was very popular. In 1883 long love-locks and shoulder curls were still in vogue. In the middle eighties, the low coil on the nape of the neck ceased to be worn, the back hair being drawn fairly high up on the top of the head. The front fringe was still fashionable (see Figs. 181 and 182). In 1890 there was a fashion for dressing the front hair in masses of little curls, and this curly dome-shaped coiffure remained in vogue for some time. For evening wear the hair was further embellished by the addition of an aigrette. In the middle nineties the back hair was brought down lower again. The 'Illustrated London News' of 1895 commented on the new Paris fashion of hairdressing. 'This consists of parting the hair in the middle, crimping it in loose curves and bringing it well down over the temples and drawn back to the ears, and arranged over a little pad as a "*bun*" behind'. Sometimes, however, the front hair was merely left to form an informal fringe (see Plate XXVI). In 1896 the 'bun', or coil of back hair, was often brought higher up on the back of the head in pseudo-1830 style, but the really characteristic coiffure of the late nineties is shown in Fig. 172. Throughout this decade, the position of the back hair underwent frequent changes. In the middle nineties the hair was coiled at the back and the end formed into a loop known as the '*teapot handle*'. Fig. 196 shows a typical coiffure of 1897, complete with '*doormat fringe*'. In 1899 the bun was worn high up on top of the head (see Fig. 197). At the same time the front hair was sometimes drawn up from the forehead to form what was termed a '*Pompadour*' front. Pads of hair and wire called 'Pompadours' were used under the hair. A fashionable coiffure of 1900 is shown in Plate XXVII.

GLOVES were worn on almost every occasion, and their absence was deemed to show a complete lack of breeding. No self-respecting woman would have dreamt of partaking of a cup of tea or sitting in a theatre with her hands uncovered. In the nineties long kid gloves were worn with evening gowns, reaching half-way between elbow and shoulder. JEWELLED BRACELETS of all kinds were very fashionable and often worn over long gloves, but the vogue for velvet wrist-bands had gone out entirely. A velvet NECK-RIBBON was still sometimes worn, and the 'Graphic' of 1898 recommended for evening wear two narrow black velvet ribbons at the throat studded with diamonds. DIAMOND TIARAS and DOG-COLLAR NECKLACES were much worn during the nineties by those who could afford them as well as elaborate DIAMOND SPRAYS for the corsage. The 'Illustrated London News' of 1895 notes the use of old-fashioned long GOLD CHAINS to support either MUFFS or LORGNETTES.[1] The gold-handled *lorgnette* gave the final touch to many a smart toilette, even when the wearer was far from being short-sighted (see Plate XXVII). FUR and FEATHER BOAS were much worn during this period (see Fig. 188), and LACE SCARVES were a useful accompaniment to evening-dress. The old-fashioned tightly-packed posy had gone out of fashion. 'SHOWER-BOUQUETS' were usually employed in the

---

[1] Pince-nez were not used until after 1846.

nineties for Royal Drawing Rooms and wedding ceremonies. FANS were popular throughout this period, and the silk or lace variety were about twelve inches in length. A fashion-writer of 1891 commented on the vogue for *ostrich-feather fans* (which were of varying sizes), and in 1893 black lace fans and hand-painted gauze fans were very fashionable. PARASOLS and UMBRELLAS were of various shapes and materials. A fashion-paper of 1880 advertised the use of *Japanese sunshades*. In 1886 the 'Graphic' notes that sunshades were very elaborate, trimmed with lace and ribbon bows and ends. During the nineties they had exceptionally long sticks known as *En-tout-cas*. In 1892, frilled parasols were popular. In fact throughout this period, the fashion-journals were full of descriptions of elaborate sunshades specially designed to accompany garden-party and other frocks.

STAGE COSTUME. During this period Henry Irving's fame increased and he became the premier actor of the English stage. His productions of 'costume' plays at the Lyceum Theatre, in which he was associated with Seymour Lucas (1849–1923) and Philip Burne-Jones, were of exceptional interest. Irving was the first of a multitudinous array of theatrical knights. He was 'dubbed' in 1895 and died in harness in 1905. To mention his colleague, the divine Ellen Terry (1848–1928) is almost superfluous.

Towards the close of his career Sir Henry had a serious rival in the production of historical plays in the person of Herbert Beerbohm Tree (1854–1917). The archæological exactitude presented by this actor-manager in his productions, including many of Shakespeare's plays, at Her Majesty's Theatre, has since aroused much conflicting criticism. It seems only fair to point out that such eminent artists as Alma-Tadema (1836–1912) and Percy Anderson (1851–1928) were among those who were entrusted with the costumes and scenery.

In the eighties and nineties Sir Augustus Harris directed the Theatre Royal, Drury Lane, producing there many spectacular plays and pantomimes, the costumes for which were designed by C. Wilhelm (C. William Pitcher, 1859–1925). This artist was also responsible for the dressing of the Empire Ballets, renowned throughout the nineties for their originality and beauty. He also costumed the first eight operas of the Gilbert and Sullivan series.

During the nineties George Alexander (1859–1918) was considered the best tailored actor on the English stage. His productions of modern comedies by Oscar Wilde (1856–1900), Arthur Wing Pinero (b. 1855) and others were noted for being extremely well dressed. Fashion once again received inspiration from the clothes worn on the stage. Society flocked to the Theatre Royal, Haymarket, and the St. James's Theatre to devour the latest mode.   It was under George Alexander's manage-ment that Mrs. Patrick Campbell took London by storm in *The Second Mrs. Tanqueray*, 1893.

AN EPILOGUE TO THE CENTURY

It is interesting to note that when, in July 1900, Queen Victoria received the 'Christian Endeavour' delegation in the quadrangle at Windsor Castle, she was dressed entirely in white; white dress, white cashmere shawl, and white hat trimmed with white ostrich-feathers. This, her first appearance out of mourning since the death of 'Albert the Good', was a fitting climax to the nineteenth century and an unconscious gesture to the dawn of a new century.

LIST OF ARTISTS WORKING AT THIS PERIOD

Lawrence Alma-Tadema	1836 1912
Edward John Poynter	1836–1919
Luke Fildes	1843–1927
Walter Crane	1845–1915
Harry Furness	1854–1925
John Singer Sargent	1856–1925
Philip Burne-Jones	1861–1926
Phil May	1864–1903
Charles Dana Gibson	1867–

GENERAL INDEX
AND
INDEX OF NAMES

GENERAL INDEX

Note:—For names of individuals and places, see Index of Names, p. 261.

253

INDEX OF NAMES